Stories from the Edge

Other books by Jimmy Santiago Baca

Poetry

Selected Poems/Poemas Selectos
Rita and Julia
Spring Poems Along the Rio Grande
Winter Poems Along the Rio Grande
C-Train and Thirteen Mexicans
Healing Earthquakes
Que Linda La Brisa/How Beautiful the Breeze Is
Immigrants in Our Own Land
Black Mesa Poems
Martin and Meditations on the South Valley

Short Stories and Essays

Adolescents on the Edge / Stories from the Edge
Working in the Dark
The Importance of a Piece of Paper
Breaking Bread with Darkness

Novel

A Glass of Water

Memoir

A Place to Stand

Film

Blood In/Blood Out
Late Blossoms
Lost Voices
Moving the River Back Home

Stories from the Edge

Jimmy Santiago Baca

HEINEMANN
Portsmouth, NH

Heinemann
361 Hanover Street
Portsmouth, NH 03801–3912
www.heinemann.com

Offices and agents throughout the world

Acknowledgments for borrowed material can be found on page vi.

Library of Congress Cataloging-in-Publication Data
Baca, Jimmy Santiago.
    Stories from the edge / Jimmy Santiago Baca.
        p. cm.
    "Accompanying grades 6–12 teacher's book, "Adolescents on the edge," and to be used in classrooms in conjunction with this volume for students."
    ISBN-10: 0-325-02948-2
    ISBN-13: 978-0-325-02948-1
    1. Special education—United States. 2. Children with disabilities—Education—United States. 3. Children with social disabilities—Education—United States. 4. Learning disabled children—Education—United States. 5. Short stories, American. 6. People with disabilities in literature.   I. Baca, Jimmy Santiago, Adolescents on the edge.   II. Title.
    LC4015.B26 2010
    371.9'0473—dc22   2010000958

Editor: Lisa Luedeke
Production: Vicki Kasabian
Cover design: Lisa A. Fowler
Cover photography: Steven St. John Photography
Typesetter: Publishers' Design and Production Services, Inc.
Manufacturing: Valerie Cooper

Printed in the United States of America on acid-free paper
14 13 12 11 10   VP   1 2 3 4 5

Contents

The authors and publisher wish to thank those who have generously given permission to reprint borrowed material:

Excerpts from "An Interview with Santiago Baca" by Frederick Luis Aldama originally appeared in *MELUS: Journal of the Society for the Study of the Multi-Ethnic Literature of the United States*, issue 30.3 (Fall 2005), pages 113–27. Reprinted by permission of the publisher.

Excerpts from "Jimmy Santiago Baca Interview" by Barbara Stahura originally appeared in *The Progressive*, January 2006, Volume 67, No. 1. Reprinted by permission of the publisher.

Excerpts from "'Sucked into a Shooting Star': A Conversation with Jimmy Santiago Baca" by Jean Cheney originally appeared in *Human Ties, Utah Humanities Council Newsletter*, Fall 2009. Reprinted by permission of the Utah Humanities Council.

Excerpts from "Interview with Jimmy Santiago Baca" by Elizabeth Farnsworth from *The NewsHour with Jim Lehrer*, August 9, 2001. Copyright © 2001 by MacNeil/Lehrer Productions. Reprinted by permission of MacNeil/Lehrer Productions.

Introduction

The Journey to Be Loved

I've written more extensively about this in my memoir *A Place to Stand*, but I'd like to give you a snapshot of how it all started—that is, how I learned to read and write when I was in my twenties, and what the journey was like.

The first five years of my life were enveloped in a sweet silence of the prairie and so abundant was silence that I could lose myself for hours playing with pieces of wood, stones, and flowers. The wind whispered to me, shadows urged me to follow them into darker spaces in abandoned barns and shacks. I hurled headlong into the depth of light that shone with a dull density in the grasshopper's wings, and it seemed a solitary angel's voice sang all my wounds open and squeezed from them the infection and healed my pain by morning's end.

With my imagination so intact and volatile, casting on inanimate things a vigorous life of their own, I was anything but lonely. All things reflected their dreams to me, and induced in me a hypnotic enchantment where I re-created and shaped my perspective on life.

If I saw an old man pushing a cart of pots and pans he had repaired and was trying to sell, he became a prince giving away secret maps to the fabled fairy-tale lands. A grasshopper became God in green wings and large eyes and antennae. A horny toad, a warrior armored for battle. Ants were my serfs and I whirled in the dust and cacti crawling in the dirt trying to scare a quail. I became Pavarotti, singing in my own romantic opera on a stage inhabited by cedar and juniper trees that sat spellbound listening to my tragic and ecstatic tale.

I compressed all life into a common pebble that I tossed in the air and pocketed because I liked its colors or markings.

It was all pretending because pretending was a way to deny seeing my dad and mom fight last night. My own make-believe world blocked out the other world of drunk uncles and money-hungry cousins and fights about poverty.

It was when I was five years old, after my parents had left us with grandma, that grandma said she could not take care of my sister, brother, and me and she informed us that authorities would arrive within days to take my brother and me to an orphanage.

With that information my pretend world shattered.

But it wasn't as bad as I expected.

I learned to understand a new reality through the eyes of movie characters like Pinocchio, Bambi, and Ben-Hur, and in the classroom at the orphanage, I would sit by the window and doodle in the margins of my Dick and Jane book. I never learned to read very well and my ability to express myself was negligible at best. Books had very little to do with my life for the first eighteen years.

I was an impulsive, idealistic follower. I thought everyone had the answer to how the world really worked except me. I was wrong but I didn't know it because everyone seemed opinionated and boasted about their wisdom. I'd go with anyone to do almost anything they asked; as long as they led, I was their guy, there to give support and show my loyalty.

The orphanage was run by Franciscan nuns and they didn't put much importance on education, at least not as much as converting our souls and making sure we grew into pious Christians.

I enjoyed enormously singing in the choir, and I belted out Latin lyrics to hymns as if the good Lord sat a foot away from me midair listening to my beautiful homage. I loved working the barn animals, milking the cows, feeding the pigs, riding the back of trucks, and going around town picking up donated shoes and day-old donuts and bread; wrecking havoc on the playground with our incredibly dangerous games.

But I had problems with saints. Kneeling in the pews every morning and praying to them? Ugh. Especially knowing that Father Gallagher was molesting certain kids, and some of the younger nuns were carrying on sexual liaisons with other kids. And then there were the gruesome Stations of the Cross that flanked the pews and hung on the walls surrounding us.

All this made me wonder about the world and confused me even more. Still, I endured the discrepancies and lounged in my happiness like an old dog before a fireplace in winter. That is, until Sister Pauline, the Superior, informed me she was sending me to Boys Town.

I ran away that same evening. I begged my older brother to come with me but he was scared, so I hugged him, and he stood there looking after me as I disappeared into the night. Had I known at the time I would not see my brother for a year after that night, I probably wouldn't have left him.

Not knowing a person in the world beyond the fence boundary of the orphanage, nor anything about the world beyond, I clambered over the fence, and crawled on hands and knees until I was far enough away to stand and run along the ditch. I headed in the direction where I thought my maternal grandma lived.

I found her place but she had been moved and I was homeless. I became a street kid for the next seven years, joined a group of other homeless kids, going in and out of the Boys Detention

Home, doing time at Montessa Park—a gladiator school that prepared teenagers for prison—and months at different intervals in
the county jail for fighting, burglary, and possession of drugs.

It was a small leap to prison. On the cusp of turning nineteen,
I was convicted of possession of heroin with the intent to sell and
sentenced to five to ten years in a maximum-security prison without chance of parole, to do day for day with no good time allowed.

I was physically stopped and I needed to be; if I hadn't been,
I am absolutely certain I'd be dead. I was on a death mission for
years, partying, getting drunk, doing drugs, hanging out with the
wrong guys—in every respect, when I look back on those days, I
see a kid, yes—innocent and beautiful and lost and uneducated
and with no family or real friends, and because of that, with a
hidden suicide wish.

In prison, however, I wanted to change that and get an education and see if I could improve my life, even from behind bars and
walls. But the prison administration refused to let me attend
school to get my GED and I retaliated by refusing to work or go
along with the prison rules. This branded me as a troublemaker.
I was given indefinite disciplinary punishment and locked down
in administrative segregation, in a dungeon with the most brutal
and cruelest gangbangers, where for the next three years I taught
myself to read and write.

I wanted to learn to read and write because it was a tool that
would help me understand people and systems—why people do
what they do. Why was it that my family was so poor and dys-
functional? What mechanism was in the system that a judge
wouldn't even consider giving me a chance to help myself? Why,
when looking through the bars of my prison cell, was it that all
those people were free and I was not? Books had the answers, and
I was going to find them. I was determined to solve my dilemma

myself. I had depended on what people said and suggested for far too long. Now, my life and my role in the world would be shaped and molded by my own ideas and feelings.

The driving force to educate myself never slowed or relented. I devoured books. I wrote my first letters to people, I kept a journal, wrote poems, and miraculously the power of literacy took hold and dug in and embedded itself in my heart. I became known to myself and loved who I started to know in me. Through the mist and darkness, through the tears and misguided intentions, through the anger and despair that entangled me for so many years, Jimmy was emerging—a strong, beautiful Jimmy, with the growing capacity to think and analyze the world beyond, and to make courageous choices interacting in that world.

It was extraordinary to have this power to name things, to study my past and understand why I did what I did. The destructive forces at play in my life stopped and positive and creative forces poured in, transforming me into a formidable human being capable of healing old wounds and forgiving enemies. Every morning on awaking, I eagerly moved forward into a new landscape where a future awaited me.

I was not going to be exiled like a leper or driven from society like a low-life criminal. I was not a criminal, I was a human being trying to understand the world, and I learned I could not do it without educating myself. As a human being, I suffered through horrible times where I almost gave up. I couldn't go anymore—I wanted to pick up old habits and resume my violent response to the world. Someone disrespected me, stole something of mine, said something bad to me and I found myself wanting to throw the books away and deal with the punk on the yard and show him you don't earn a reputation with me so other convicts will look up to you—no, you get a beat-down.

But I realized this was the coward's way, and this way never worked for me. Now, I realized, I had an opportunity to give myself a fighting chance to make my dreams come true and I went for it, with as much gusto and fearlessness as I ever had going for anything I'd wanted in my past life.

It was all going to be different now and I was going to make it happen myself. If I had to pace my cell for twenty years to learn how to read, I would do it. Thank God it didn't take that long. Restlessly, when I started I paced for hours in my cell reading aloud, writing on a tablet for hours, reading all through the night, month after month, until finally, I could compose my first letter.

Not only did I go through enormous changes, but suddenly the hard-core fighters and warriors around me started looking at me and treating me with renewed respect. They wanted me to speak for them, to answer their questions, and help them solve their problems by helping them understand their own feelings.

I remember with joy what an incredible power it was to be able to express myself, not just read and write, but convey my ideas to another convict, to have their respect because I was smart, to have them depend on me to write their letters home, to have them look up to me because I had done it, improved myself, done something they wanted to do but felt they couldn't do.

I never suspected in my craziest reveries that I would eventually become a poet. Nor could I allow myself to imagine that the poems I was writing down in the dungeon would be published one day.

I had my first book of poems published by Louisiana State University and shortly after that one, ten more books followed. I wrote and executive-produced *Blood In/Blood Out*, the feature movie produced by Hollywood Pictures. I went on to write novels, short story collections, more poetry, essays, more movies. But as important as all of this is, including my thirty-two awards, rising above all these achievements, is that I am now educated. I went to school, got my BA and master's, and was honored with a PhD.

And greater than even that, I have a lovely family, and my five children are very proud of and love their father. That was all I ever wanted, to be respected and loved.

Stories
from
the Edge

The Swing Test That Made Us Men

It was a test alright and it cut the boys from the men. At the orphanage, there were only two swings for twelve hundred kids and every kid on the playground yearned for the opportunity to ride the swing because it symbolized much more than just a swing.

First of all, you had to earn your turn. When a kid was carted off or simply tired of swinging, everyone raced to get it. Lee Walker was the fastest kid in the orphanage so he had no trouble getting to it first.

The only problem was he was running out of bones to break.

Let me explain. Say you got to the swing first. You had to pump your legs and thrust your shoulders forward to get as high as you could. There was absolutely no compromise when it came to height, and once you reached the highest point in your swing, you had to bail out. You bailed out a few times like a jet pilot testing his parachute, and then went for a flip.

Don't kid yourself—every boy on the playground had their antennae tuned to you and they were clocking your every move and appraising the craft and style with which you flipped midair and landed.

But here was the most important part of this boyhood ceremony that gave ritual to our coming-of-age in the world—you had to break a bone. Breaking a bone was a symbol of manhood, a badge of honor; it meant you had walked through the fire to prove you were not afraid of pain. And the worse the break, the greater the courage you displayed before the hungry hordes of kids starving for a shot at the swing to prove themselves, too.

But there was another reason. Breaking a bone was important because only then could you join other warriors in the infirmary and get a hug from Sister Theobaldus. She was this huge three hundred and fifty–pound German nun and nestling your head between her enormous breasts was the closest thing to mothering most of us kids would ever know. In short, her breasts were Heaven on Earth and kids were willing to risk life and limb for a moment between God's gift to homeless kids.

Once we made it to the infirmary and indulged in the luxurious dream-bosom, we were in store for another treat—the lemon drop candies. Sister Theobaldus reached her massive paw into her apron pocket and pulled out a gob of lemon drops, which we all believed hastened our healing.

And while we sucked on lemon drops and grazed against the white nurse's uniform containing the eighth wonder of the world, Sister Theobaldus helped us into our pajamas and settled us into one of the beds.

There, we could relax in newfound glory among those in the other beds, feeling for a few days like one of the luckiest kids in the world.

The Magic Marble

When it was announced that a marble tournament was to be held and that the champion would go on to the regional competition, and if he advanced, then on to the state finals, my friends and I sat in the ditch away from the others and dreamed ourselves the marble champs.

We crushed dry leaves and rolled them in comic book paper into cigarettes and smoked them. We were big guys even at seven, a month or so from being adults. It was either Peanut Head or Big Noodle who came up with a plan on how to achieve our dream.

In short, we figured Cavalo's glass eye would do it for us; that is, we simply had to direct it into the ring and it would knock the marbles out of the circle. We thought the glass eye could see the marbles and so would never miss. We would not only win, we would make history and the Guinness Book of World Records for the most marbles ever hit without a miss.

But how to get the eye from Cavalo?

Cavalo was a medieval dragon of a man. There were four brand-new dorms recently built, 100s for the toddlers and infants; 200s for the slightly older, 300 and 400s for older boys. My friends and I were in the 300s, and Cavalo also slept in this dorm.

He got up earlier than us kids, trudged like one of Solzhenitsyn's Russian peasant prisoners in the semidark to the subterranean boiler room and stoked the fires to get the radiators knocking to warm the classrooms before school. Sometimes I would pass the boiler room and catch a glimpse of him below—a grizzly ogre, with Popeye forearms, hair stiff and bristly as barbwire, a permanent scowl on his face, and a perennial stream of yellowish mucus dripping from the glass eye socket.

Last time he glowered when he glanced up at me, and it scared me enough that I made it a point to avoid passing the boiler room for months.

Every night, Cavalo took his glass eye out and placed it in a glass of water on his bed stand next to his cot. With his eye out, he looked fierce, the eyelids of his socket shrunken back into tight whorls of flesh seamed with mucus.

But we did have to get that eye and the marble tournament was drawing near.

We decided that we would wait until he went to sleep and crawl over to his bed and pluck the glass eye from the water. He could always get another glass eye and we would win the tournament and, as they say, all's well that ends well.

The kids in the dorms finally went to bed and the nun who had her own enclosed room in a corner of the dorm said good night and turned off the lights. We waited a good hour until we could hear kids snoring, farting, and moaning.

Big Noodle and Coo-Coo Clock crept over to my bunk. Soon Peanut Head arrived and they all took their stations as planned. Coo-Coo Clock was posted at Sister Juanita's room and ready to alert us if he heard her moving about. Big Noodle and Peanut Head stationed themselves at the head of the bunk rows as lookouts.

I crawled over to Cavalo's cot, dipped my fingers into the glass, and scooped out the magic glass eye. I turned and saw a blurred object sailing past me and attributed the blue, dark object to my own imagination. As everyone knows, your sight plays tricks on you in the dark.

Anyway, it wasn't my imagination, it was a boot that someone had hurled through the air and it hit Cavalo in the head. He
roused from his sleep and rose out of bed in a mean roar, growl-
ing for his eye. Sister Juanita awoke and came out and turned on
the dorm light, and I froze as Cavalo loomed over me like a
mythic one-eyed giant.

He bent down and his face came within inches of mine.
"WHERE'S MY EYE?!" he bellowed.

Just before the lights had gone on I had managed, as much as
I was repulsed by it, to put the eye in my mouth. I had no choice.
I intended to spit it out later but it didn't work out that way.

Cavalo scared me so much, I swallowed it.

Sister Juanita pulled me by the ear into the bathroom where
for the next hour she made me swallow saltwater and puke, puke
at least a hundred times, until the marble came rolling out onto
the floor.

So much for the marble tournament. As punishment we had
to wash all five hundred windows in the buildings, and we missed
the tournament. I still wonder from time to time who threw that
boot.

Wells Market

There wasn't a day that passed that I didn't yearn for a visit from my mother or grandmother. During ordinary days, it was bad enough that they had never visited me, but when holidays rolled around, my longing intensified because it was a time when many families came to visit other kids in the orphanage.

At Christmastime there was so much festive excitement in the air that I couldn't sleep. I woke at 5:00 AM to attend mass after a fitful night of tossing and turning, and my first thought as my eyes lifted to greet the daylight was, *Is today the day my mother or grandmother are coming to see me?*

Still, with hope nestled in my heart on the verge of bursting forth from its star shell, I lunged into the pre-Christmas craziness at St. Anthony's orphanage.

It was the coolest holiday of all, not only because the nuns decked out the chapel with a thousand mythic candles and wreaths and freshly cut flowers, but also because mass services were rendered in Latin and I got to sing in the choir and blast out Gregorian chants, which I absolutely loved. I knew if I sang loud enough, God would hear me and grant my wish for a visit.

In the classroom, I drew and cut out snowflakes, snowmen, and Santas and taped them to the windows, spraying white snow hills for sleighs to ride over, stringing up lightbulbs, and running glittering blue and red bunting around the window frames.

We'd make and sell hundreds of *farolitos*, paper lunch sacks we'd fill with two scoops of sand and a small candle placed on top. People lined them on fence tops, rooftops, and walkways and on Christmas Eve they lit the candles. It transformed the night into a biblical fairy tale.

The chilly days smacked with excitement, games, and the flavor of special holiday foods. I had a cardboard flap I'd torn off a box and each afternoon I lined up with other kids to slide on the ice that covered the courtyard cobblestone.

In the auditorium we played the game Murder in the Dark. In this game, a ball made of old socks is set on the floor between the two teams. The object is to grab the sock ball and carry it over the opponent's line, called the end zone. This would be easy in itself, but you have to do it as someone flicks the lights on and off. If you're caught moving when the lights are on, you're out. The excitement of the game came when the lights were off. You could punch and slug and push some kid you didn't like but when the lights went on many of us were busted in the act of hitting or being hit.

When not playing Murder in the Dark, we got to watch movies like *Ben-Hur*, *Big Valley*, *Miracle on 57th Street*, and *The Christmas Story*, with Charlton Heston parting the Red Sea, and the three kings following a star to find baby Jesus asleep in the manger. And when the auditorium wasn't being used to watch movies, the nuns provided entertainment for us by inviting special guests.

A sorority from the University of New Mexico visited once. Instead of luxuriating in the attention and playing dumb games, I wanted more exciting distractions, so me and a few other pirates headed up to the condemned third floor of the main building, where the girls had stashed their coats and purses.

We felt we had beached on an island of lost treasures as we scavenged through their purses, dumping out the contents and pocketing lipsticks, panties, photos, nylons, money, and other precious valuables that could be used for barter with other kids and the nuns.

There were some nuns who would kiss us for candy, others who would dance with us for a mascara case; still others, if we brought them a new pair of nylons, invited us to their rooms at night. No matter what form it materialized in, we were starved for female affection and we found it in the young nuns who were also famished for intimacy, even if they had to compromise and engage with a boy younger than they might have wished for.

After we had pillaged the coat and purse room, taken the loot to the barn and hidden it under the haystack, we returned to the auditorium. I should have listened to my friends' warning not to bring anything inside but I couldn't help it—I was a show-off.

I brought back a purse to show the other kids how special I was, how brave and bad I was. After showing it to a few kids and getting what I wanted—a bunch of blazing *ooob*s and *wow*s, their eyes wide with admiration conferring heroic status on me— I stuffed the evidence behind a radiator and, intent on getting it later, forgot about it.

The stench of melting plastic filled the auditorium and soon smoke rose from behind the radiator. One of the nuns plucked out a half-melted purse and demanded to know who the guilty one was. Meanwhile, the sorority girls had rushed out of the auditorium to check on their belongings and returned aghast over the burglary.

The nuns lined us up and sternly paced back and forth with arms crossed behind their backs. They wanted an admission of guilt, and ordered the immediate return of the purses and con-tents, threatening to punish everyone if the guilty party didn't step forward.

I confessed, but I didn't tell them that I had saved a bunch of lipsticks and mascara cases for my mother in case she came dur-ing Christmas to see me. I put them in a special hiding place. And when they sent the older boys to retrieve our stash, I was pleased that I had something left to redeem a bit of the pain from the beating that was coming.

Room Number 5 was the hated and feared room where kids were sent to get a spanking. I had visited there many times. I had been there for raiding the kitchen cart when it came rumbling down the long hallway toward the dining room, and my friends and I would leap down from the staircase and load up on the hot-dogs and cake and butter. Other times I was caught stuffing myself with cherry-filled chocolates, extorted from nuns carrying on secret affairs with kids. But mostly I was punished for the many times I had run away to see my grandma.

I ran to my grandma because I knew where she was, whereas my mother's life was a mystery. My mother had vanished into thin air and I was never told where she lived or what she was doing. But I was certain she would come for me; I figured she was planning our reunion just as I was.

After the stinging from the spanking numbed and I could tod-dle again, I walked into the chapel at five o'clock as we did every morning. Besides the lipsticks and mascara I had saved for my mother, the chapel with its wreaths, candles, serene nativity scene, and the singing of Christmas hymns in the choir loft seemed to alleviate my soreness.

I couldn't wait to be outside again, on my knees in the sand pile bagging *farolitos*, snapping out a paper sack and pouring in two scoops of sand and a candle, loading up the civilian trunks of endless cars waiting to purchase enough sacks to decorate their houses. Then, we would ride all over the city in the back of the truck, emptying the endless parking-lot containers of donations to the orphanage, and ride back on a mountain of shoes or clothes piled in the back of the truck. Some days we'd hit bakeries and grocery stores and load the truck with pastries and bread;

other days we'd hit farmer's markets and load the truck with blemished fruits.

But no matter the excursions and adventure, to alleviate my worrisome yearning for my mother, I snuck into Father Gallagher's rectory and drank wine, and when I got drunk enough, I stole a few holy wafers from the chalice in his rectory and ate them as I promised eternal devotion to God if he only brought my mom to visit me.

But my mother never came.

Perhaps it was jumping into the arctic swimming pool in the morning during winter that made my immune system so resilient, or playing with Lincoln Logs in the playroom and napping on the floor with a cold draft coming under the doors, or playing on the teeter–totter while it was snowing, or baseball during windy days, or any number of other things I did. But as immune as I was, my heart still felt the touch of sorrow and folded in on itself like a butterfly's time to die in winter, curled up to endure its own solitude during such a communally happy time.

Months earlier, I had run away from the orphanage to plunder gifts that I intended to give to my grandma. To break into a secondhand store with nice hats, I had climbed up to the roof using the fire escape stairwell, kicked out the air-conditioning ductwork, and slid into the store. Once in, I loaded up on dresses, shoes, hats, and panties for my grandma, then threw the bag holding everything up through the hole I'd made in the ceiling and leaped after it. Grabbing the sides of the ceiling, I kicked my legs up and hooked my feet over the edge.

Just as I was ready to pull myself up, a police cruiser pulled up and two officers entered. They swept the place with their flashlights and, satisfied everything was okay, prepared to leave when the pennies I had stuffed in my pocket from the cash register began raining down on the floor. Their strobe lights swept the dark again until they found the waterfall of pennies and trailed it up to me, hanging upside down like a monkey, my eyes staring down at them.

They had arrested me before for running away and that night they were the ones who told me that my grandmother had been taken to a place for old people, where she would be tended to because she was too old and couldn't take care of herself. They said she had a disease called Alzheimer's, but it wasn't hurting her. They took me to see where she was living, but we only passed by the place. I wasn't allowed inside.

When the other kids' grandmothers came to visit them, I waited day after day at the outside gate by the Virgin Mary Grotto hoping my grandma might drive up with a bag of holiday goodies too, but that never happened.

Once, I went with my friend Coo-Coo Clock to the Blue Room, the room for visits, and I saw him and his grandmother and others in their chairs. The kids were unwrapping new head scarves, slipping on new gloves and coats, and piled on their laps were bags filled with toys and candies. My friends shared their candies with me, but it wasn't the same as having a family member visit.

It was maybe a week from Christmas, when the nuns got us all together and bused us to the zoo park to play.

When the teams were chosen for a football game, I was selected by one of the most popular kids in the orphanage—Johnny La'O. He was the biggest and strongest and everybody feared him, even though he was nice and seldom threw his weight around. He was not a bully; he was as compassionate and heroic as Ben-Hur was in the black-and-white movies we watched on Friday nights in the auditorium.

Anyway, he chose me, and I guess knowing that I didn't have anyone visit me for Christmas, he looked directly at me in the huddle and said he was going to throw the bomb to me. That meant a long Hail Mary pass.

And I was going to catch it and run for a touchdown. At least that was what I had imagined would happen.

When the football was hiked I dashed as fast as I could, as far as my little legs would carry me and I turned and saw the football sailing my way. My entire focus was on it. Catching it was the only thing that mattered in the whole world. I reached out and I had it. Within seconds, I imagined myself galloping for a touchdown, then lofted on my teammates' shoulders as they carried me victoriously to our team bench.

Instead, everything went black.

In a tiny, white room, my spirit hovered over an operating room lamp, observing doctors below. There they stood, working on my physical body, which was reclined on an operating gurney while the doctors wrapped my head in gauze and the nuns surrounding me clasped hands, clutching rosaries as they prayed.

Disembodied, I was floating in a space with no time or place. I had just been operated on. And I heard words like *coma* and *chin* and *tree* and phrases about God saving me. Looking down at myself, I wondered how I got on the gurney and into the hospital. I wasn't worried, I was curious.

That out-of-body experience was only temporary, perhaps because I was so heavily medicated. I'm still puzzled by how I ended up back at the orphanage. But there I was, hours or days later—I can't remember—standing in line with the other kids with a huge gauze bandage circling my head. The gauze was wrapped under my chin too, and I looked like a huge, walking marshmallow.

I don't remember much about that time, except it was close to Christmas and I wanted to see my grandma, the only person in the world besides my mother who made living a magical experience, and who could redeem the perpetual, throbbing misery I was in. I would willingly, even gratefully, accept the sorrow of life if I'd just be allowed to see my grandma once a year during Christmas.

A week later I was in line in the auditorium when Santa came and gave out red stockings stuffed with fruits and nuts and a few *ho-ho-ho*s. I could tell he was a fake Santa because I could see the beard bands and the discolored hair under his hat. He had yellow teeth, red-veined eyes from drinking too much the night before, and lint caught in the hair tufts around his ears.

After Santa left we all lined up again to meet three huge black men, ushered in by the nuns with pontifical decorum. Each kid shook the hand of the one giant flanked by two smaller ones and moved on until my turn came and the black giant leaned down and bellowed in a baritone voice, "What happened little buddy? Somebody hit you?"

I shook my head no and wanted to say I ran into a tree but I couldn't move my mouth or jaw that well. His interest pleased me. He gently caressed my chin with a big, black, thick finger, then turned to one of his two assistants beside him and said, "Joe, go to the car and bring the gloves."

His errand man came right back and gave these two big red boxing gloves to him.

In a voice low as a paddle in water, he leaned down and said, "My name is Sonny Liston. I am the heavyweight champion of the world. I won the title fight with these gloves. They have magic; they can help you win fights, make you a winner, a champion. Here."

He held the gloves out to me.

They were as big as my torso, shoulders, and arms, and I hugged them to me like they were real teddy bears. I took a chair in the auditorium with the other kids, and sensed these gloves were big business; they meant something big.

Johnny La'O came up behind me and whispered, "I'll give you whatever you want for those, Jimmy, anything," he said. Then added, with passion, "Please . . . *please.*"

I thought for a second and then I uttered with great difficulty, "I-want-to-see-my-grandma . . . and-you-can-have-the-gloves."

That night, when everyone was asleep in the dorm, as arranged between Johnny La'O and me and following his instructions, I snuck out and ran to the fields by the public road. There, I waited in the alfalfa until I heard a motorcycle drive up and idle by the road shoulder and field.

I dashed to the motorcycle and hopped on the back and the driver took off.

"Where to?" he yelled back at me.

I used my hands to motion him directions until we arrived at the old folks' house where my grandma was living. He parked and we went inside.

At first I was kind of disoriented because I had never seen her in this place. The police had driven me by, but I had never been in.

Tonight, I went inside and I saw my grandma in the corner. She was the only white-skinned woman; the rest were old blacks, kind of lounging and ambling aimlessly, standing and lolling, moving slowly to nowhere.

I approached my grandma. "Grandma, Grandma . . ." I called her even though it hurt my head to speak.

She turned and squinted at me. After a moment she blurted out angrily, "Get away! You stole everything, get away! Get out!"

She was referring to her own children, and she called me by the name of one of her older sons. They had stripped her of her land and money and thrown her into this old-age hell-home.

She swung and hit me with her cane. Then swung and hit me again.

I was so hurt that a part of me recoiled in horror and I wanted to end the world. I wanted to rewind my life and before it started, light a match that would burn the world down. This was my pain, but instead of the world burning outside, inside my head my world was a burnt and charcoaled landscape where only night existed and ashes blew continually under the blood red moon called my heart.

My friend tugged at my arm and told me, "Let's go! Let's go! She's going to hit you on the chin and that's going to be bad— she doesn't know who you are Jimmy, she's insane, she's gone crazy."

I followed him out. I felt like throwing up, like I had swallowed poison.

We got on the bike and returned to the orphanage.

The next day, Johnny La'O, knowing what happened, said he had a surprise for me.

I met him on the playground and he led me across the fields, away from the orphanage. I thought we were running away together, that we were going to live with the many girlfriends he had out there on the streets.

But we weren't.

We entered Wells Market, a store as famous in the imagination of children as the North Pole at Christmas. Very rarely did the kids ever make it this far away from the orphanage, and even fewer got to go inside Wells, a storybook store with legendary shelves of candies that blinded one's heart to all else in life.

Only the older kids risked their lives to come to Wells Market, and on their return all we youngsters ringed them as they talked about the aisles brimming with exotic toys and candies.

Now, I saw, and it was true. The store contained all the candies in the world, the shining jewels that sparkled in every kid's dreams.

When I left Wells Market that afternoon, carrying a paper sack filled with fizzies, lollipops, chips, gum, and much more, I was reeling with unspeakable joy. I was numb with ecstasy.

Sure, other kids had parents and homes and grandmas, but now *I* had been to Wells Market. Word got around fast. I was the most famous kid in the world that day. Kids mobbed me as a hero—I had made the perilous journey and returned safe, laden with gold and stories of high adventure, stories that I made up about almost being shot by a rabid farmer protecting his chili garden and how I'd been chased by wild dogs.

That day, like a seasoned politician, I leveraged the candy I handed out. For two scoops, Chief, a big Navajo, let me poke Big Oscar's balls with a stick. Big Oscar was the ribbon-winning state fair champion pig, as big as a truck. Chief typically charged us a dinner dessert to poke Oscar in the balls. This activated Oscar's penis, which slid out from its black pouch of flesh. Little by little the pencil-thin penis appeared and elongated four feet out, a skinny red worm. I also bartered my way onto a go-cart team.

But the best part was being allowed admittance that night to a once-in-a-lifetime viewing of Sister Rita, a kid's girlfriend, in a bathing suit in her room. Sister Rita's room was lit up with candles, and she came out in a bathing suit and turned and smiled. I sat on the couch drooling, stuffing my mouth with candies, until she paused and sat next to me.

Then she held me in her arms like a mother and rocked me.

It was the greatest Christmas ever.

Eleven Cents

Over the years I have met dozens of women who call themselves *curanderas*—spiritual healers—but they all fell short of being truly genuine and authentic. They were usually middle-aged women claiming to be artists but secretly working through their own traumatic experiences, usually caused by a male lover. They were hapless Frida Kahlo look-alikes in long skirts and blouses, professing to be consumed by mystical connections to the spirit world.

Their aura said that their sole purpose in life was to suffer so they might heal others by sacrificing themselves. Only the curanderas were privy to the divine answers they passed on to those who came for counseling. The curandera would answer the questions and the seeker would be given direction and purpose in life.

About a year ago, I picked up two young Chicanos who work in the film industry in Los Angeles from Albuquerque's West Side and we headed down to the university area soundstage to meet a renowned curandera to participate in her blessing circle. I wanted to meet her because I had heard she had powerful prayers and it was a time in my life when I was searching for someone who could help revitalize my depressed spirit. I was intrigued by the stories I'd heard of her and secretly yearned for a genuine healer woman. I needed strong prayers in my life.

On the way there my two Chicano friends were hungry, so we pulled into Wendy's on 4th Street and called out our burger order and idled to the drive-up window.

A short, dark Mexican repeated our order and I nodded, opening my palm to take the money from my two passengers, then I handed it to the Mexican at the window.

"You're eleven cents short," he said.

The two Chicanos leaned forward to be heard better by the Mexican.

"Come on dude," Val said, "it's only eleven cents, man."

Eddy added, "Let it go. We're one people. We'd do the same for you."

"Give each other breaks, man. Don't hassle us over eleven cents."

But the Mexican was having none of it. "Nobody gave *me* a break when I came here. I went without eating for days. Nobody gave me even a piece of bread."

"Yeah," Val argued, "but that wasn't *us*. This is bull. Eleven cents? You kidding me?"

"No kidding anybody. Pay or you're not getting anything."

Eddy went into a rage, started hollering at him, "You punk! Who do you think you are? You don't even belong here in this country! Go back home, kissing up to the white man."

"You ain't nothing but a sellout, vato," Val yelled.

But he was adamant and refused to hand over the bags of fries, sodas, and burgers.

"Let me out! I'm going to show this dude how we do business here," Val said.

"Why should I give you a break?" the Mexican in the window cried out. "No one, not one person, gave me anything, nothing, when I came here, not a penny—I had to earn everything I got. No one ever gave me a hamburger. No one gave me a hamburger when I came here! No one! I had to pay for everything."

This enraged the two Chicanos even more. Any connection between his suffering and theirs, between what happened to the

Mexican when he came to America and how it mattered in this scene with the burgers and eleven cents—they couldn't see it.

I pulled eleven cents out of my pocket and handed it to him and took the bags for Val and Eddy. They grumbled at him, cursed at him, spat with disgust at his revolting subservience to the gringo boss.

I drove across the street and ordered fries, burgers, and soda from McDonald's, and then looped back and came around again to the drive-up window.

"What the hell are you doing?" the Mexican said when he saw us. "Do you have a gun? I'm not afraid of you."

"I don't have a gun. I just came back to say I'm sorry for the way you were treated when you came here. I wish it hadn't been that way. I wish you had been given respect and help. We all deserve that."

I paused and looked in his fearful eyes. "I wanted to give you this burger, fries, and soda, on me, as my way of saying I'm sorry."

Stunned, he stood there blinking and trying to register it mentally, not believing what I was saying for a second, absolutely certain that this was some kind of setup to hurt him.

"What's going on?" he said suspiciously. "You trying to pull something?"

There was no convincing him.

"I'm going to leave this here, and again I'm sorry. Have a good night."

"Whoa, whoa, what are you doing?" Val said. "I'll eat those. Don't give it to that punk."

I turned around and looked at Val.

"He's not a *punk*," I said. "You guys don't have a clue how hard it is for an immigrant to come here and start with nothing."

I placed the bag on the little stainless shelf of the drive-up window.

"Please forgive us, brother. I'm sorry," I said sincerely. And I drove off.

After a ride of deep silence, the two Chicanos said, "You're right, we're sorry brother, we're sorry . . . that was cool what you did."

And the curandera and her prayers were real.

Forgiving the Godfather of Poetry

Lamont was a very cool cat, given a sweet gift of poetry. He was a Vietnam veteran, a community activist, and my friend. No better man. A young Afro-American ahead of his time surviving on the streets of Camden, New Jersey, he spent his time teaching the youngsters there how to love themselves.

The folks over at the Walt Whitman center invited me to come and read, and afterward Lamont walked me through the night streets of Camden, sharing with me the grisly statistics—number one in crime, severe poverty, lots of black-on-black violence, illiteracy, and despair.

I have to tell you, though, the people at the Walt Whitman center were amazing. They had a powerful organization, with community outreach employees who were meeting the challenges faceup in your grill—that is, they didn't theorize, they engaged; they didn't blackboard their ideas, they worked them out; they didn't armchair the youth to death with counseling, they walked beside them in the streets.

After the reading, we hung out to chat with the people and then I said good night, and Lamont walked me back to my room. We passed a lot of addicts, a lot of gangbangers. The streets were littered and the general unkempt and disheveled look of the place might have been a telltale sign of being ignored by the city counselors, but I knew if Lamont was any proof, a lot of artists lived in these run-down Victorian clapboards and creativity was thriving. He pointed to the county jail where I would be tomorrow, conducting a writing workshop, and we said good night.

It was a cold walk down to the jail from my hotel the next morning: frost on the windows, nasty old snow banked up on the streets' curbs, drug needles, snipped-off cocaine straws, liquor bottles, and beer cans wherever I glanced.

The jail, a five-story hulk of gray block with dark barred windows mirrored the winter's misery, its bitterness punishing the morning's hope with a dreamless despair.

Inside, my shoulder bag was checked, and I was patted down, walked through the metal detector, and swept with a wand by a guard. I collected my bag and coat and followed the guard upstairs and into a classroom that overlooked the gray streets below.

In a few minutes the cons came in, blacks and Latinos, mostly Puerto Ricans and Dominicans. This was a few years back and Mexicans hadn't flooded the east coast yet; now they are equal in number to the rest of the cons.

Once I had them in their seats, I paced back and forth in the front of the room and talked about the power of reading and writing. Most were fathers, all were drug abusers, many had been homeless and in a gang, almost all were in their twenties.

I treated them with great respect, keying in on topics to reference our similar experiences, trying to illuminate certain insights to help them endure the oppression they lived in daily.

I said, "Poetry is pretty much like fishing the outer banks of the mind. Writing is all about visiting those isolated islands in our hearts and learning how to make fire with rocks."

"Like sleeping on the sand in Santo Domingo and feeling the ocean waves channel deeper and deeper into your heart," a Dominicano cried.

"Exactly, my brother," I replied. "And then imagine that sacred water flushing out every impurity in your body and heart, and imagine every molecule in your body dancing with a sweet peacefulness you've never experienced before."

"Andale!" the Dominicano cried out again.

"Baile! Baile!" a Puerto Rican added.

They loved the magical aspects of poetry.

A tall Dominican was excited by the idea of writing a poem—he said, in a beautiful, warm, honeyed, coffee baritone voice, "I want you to help me write a poem to my wife—it's our anniversary today."

"Absolutely," I said. "We will all get the fires burning."

But no matter the hope I had offered, no matter how I had whittled down their heart's despair and elevated their esteem, all my words collapsed in crushing disappointment when I asked the guard to pass out pencils and paper so we could write poetry.

The guard said they were not allowed to have pencils, some sort of consequence for a recent situation wherein a convict was stabbed to death with one.

After trying to argue for pencils with the guard on duty, I resigned myself to a Q & A, telling the cons all sorts of stories about poetry: how Coleridge was an opium addict, Jack London a racist, Walt Whitman gay, and so on. I wanted to make these famous poets human to them, and they lit up with a thousand questions.

"What is a poem?"

"It's a sincere calling on spirits to visit you and bless you with words to express your darkest secrets and most radiant dreams."

"Can it be about bad stuff?"

"The most vile and corrupt acts humans commit, poetry turns into literary gems that reflect a truth that is in all of us."

Most of the men were engaged, but not the Dominican—his thoughtful visage was imbued with memories of his wife and the things they shared and did together. Eventually, he asked the guard for permission to use the bathroom and left.

We kept on talking about poets and poetry until the guard got suspicious of the Dominican being gone so long and he left the room to check on him.

That's when the alarm rang.

"Stay put in your chairs and don't move," the guard ordered the cons. "Over to the windows against the wall and stay put," he said to me.

I wondered if the Dominican tried to escape—or maybe hit a guard or something. Maybe he got into a fight with another con. I inhaled and walked around the room alongside the wall and then went out the door to the bathroom. A guard at the bathroom door said I was not allowed in, but when I looked, I saw what the Dominican had done.

They had already taken him down to the infirmary and were wiping the blood off the walls, blood he had scooped up with his fingers after cutting himself across the wrists. Blood he had painted on the wall composing the anniversary poem to his wife.

I left the jail and walked across the street to an apartment where Walt Whitman used to live and sat on the stoop of his house thinking that life can sometimes look real bleak.

What an irony, men forbidden to have pencils and paper in this place where the greatest American poet had lived a block away. In fact, when I'd been in the jail that morning, I could clearly see his house from the window in the classroom upstairs where we sat. I had been looking down on Walt's house when the alarm had sounded.

Looking down, I might add, feeling I was part of this cruel paradox. Here was Walt, a symbol of freedom and love and compassion and a block away, overlooking his house, was a jail that housed young men society had condemned to live without any of those humane principles.

I got up and walked a few blocks to the Camden cemetery where I found Walt's grave. Sitting next to it, I thought about how he believed in the doctrine of Manifest Destiny, that America was destined, even ordained by God, to expand across the entire continent. Many of my people, Native American Mexicans, indigenous Mexicans, tribal Mexicans with roots plunging deep into pre-Columbian times, were hanged, burned out, murdered, raped, and driven off their lands in the name of this doctrine. Manifest Destiny, soaked in my people's blood as it was, advocated this. Walt Whitman believed that God had blessed this slaughter, that America should extend coast to coast, from sea to shining sea.

I dug into my satchel and pulled out the eagle feather I carried everywhere with me and a half loaf of Indian fried bread. Placing both on his grave, I prayed. Sitting at his grave that day, I forgave Walt Whitman for his belief that had so dearly cost so many of my people.

Thirty minutes later I found myself walking into an elementary school. It was to be my last gig in Camden, and then I was going home.

The school looked more like a prison for kindergarteners. Coils of razor wire wrapped around the building, and at the entrance I had to insert my hand into a slot in the wall, place my palm flat on an ink pad, and press so a machine could read my fingerprints. While this was going on, a camera mounted high above clicked a snapshot of me. Someone manning a remote control board inside unlocked the latch and a voice came through a speaker, instructing me to enter.

The first thing that hit me overwhelmingly was the smell of fresh and warm oven-baked bread. It smelled so, so good and more so in contrast to the predatory streets and sorrowful experience of the Dominican convict.

A teacher escorted me to a classroom filled with thirty wide-eyed little African American angels and I asked my first question.

"How many of you know someone who has been hurt or killed by the drug dealers I saw standing on every corner this morning?"

Every kid raised a hand.

"Why then, if coming to school means you have to risk your life," I asked, "why do you come every morning? Especially when you know there's a possibility you may never reach the school?"

Every answer was the same—*because my momma wants me to get an education.*

So they risk their lives to get an education, I thought.

And because they were expected by all statistics and environmental laws to fail, and they weren't, I felt so delighted I was swept away on the wave of their determined innocence and I yelled out, "Come on! It's monkey pile time!"

I crouched on all fours in the center of the room and I was engulfed from all sides with giggling and screaming kids, each harboring a dream to be an artist, doctor, scientist, or carpenter, kids who refused to live in fear, reeking of cheap hair tonic and soap, with snotty noses and peed underpants, yet smelling as fragrant as any queen's garden in spring to my heart.

Sign Language, Convict Style

Prisoners all over the world, be it Korea, Russia, China, Mexico, or America, have created their own unique language to communicate with each other. In many prisons, convicts are not often allowed to speak, so over many decades they have learned to use their hands, facial features, and fingers to talk to each other from cell to cell, across cellblock landings, or from barred windows to their loved ones gathered on street corners, on the sidewalks of every downtown city in the world.

They must speak by signing in the convict code.

On the bed in my room, I spread out photographs taken by James Drake. He had express mailed me a batch of photographs saying he needed me to put poems to the photographs and he wanted me to hurry. The photos and the poems were going to be exhibited at the Whitney Museum in New York.

There were photos of prisoners signing through security Plexiglas to their loved ones in visiting rooms; photos of convicts signing through windows to acquaintances on street corners below; photos of prisoners signing to each other. As I studied photos of dolled-up girlfriends on street corners, I noticed rows of bail bond offices behind them.

The women were often pretty, the men tattooed and marked by hard street life. In many pictures, couples sat close to each other and signed through thick mesh wire embedded in bulletproof glass, their eyes reflecting the painful devastation of lovers caught in the blade-net of addiction.

I noted how their fingers bent to make letters, how both hands met midair or hip high to arrange a series of words that formed a sentence. The depth and breadth, width and height that this prisoner sign language embodied to articulate their misery and needs was startling. I could tell by the faces of the signer and responder that their conversation was deep, though it could be about anything from Grandma's latest recipe to their son's problems at school.

I felt sad for this fringe group of young people so on the margins of society that they had had to create their own sign language to communicate. At the same time, I was amazed by humanity's ingenuity to adapt to adverse circumstances.

The poems and the exhibit were a great success, but later, something even better happened. I had the opportunity to test the extent of the sign language and prove it was, indeed, a real language.

I had long heard Chino was the fiercest gladiator preparatory prison for young adults in the country, and I had been looking forward to this trip to the California State Youth Authority prison at Chino, not only because I wanted to try out the theory that had crystallized in my mind from the work I had done with James Drake, but because it was the perfect prison to see if my theory was right. We had a full week to test it and I was delighted.

My interns, Efren, Karina, Valentine, and I were met in the lobby by our host, a wonderful blonde-haired woman with an outgoing vitality in her speech and gestures. She had the kind of energy that made me want to take up running and swimming so I could exude the same aura of good healthy living. With her as our host, the workshop looked promising.

After passing through a series of weapon-detector gates where guards monitored the computer screens for guns or knives, another guard gave us a going-over with a contraband wand, and still another frisked and patted each of us down. Then we were led through several halls and out a door into the most welcoming broad compound flushed with bright daylight that ever warmed one's cheeks.

Here, a man with long graying hair and a turquoise necklace met us and introduced himself as one of the counselors at the prison. He was also the facilitator for the religious ceremonies of the natives in the prison. Everyone called him Uncle Jimmy.

As it turned out, over the next five days Uncle Jimmy would be extremely kind to us. He had a low-key disposition, and one would expect given the environment that he would be serious, but his conversation was lighthearted and his treatment of the inmates stern, but evenhanded.

Uncle Jimmy gave me free rein to roam about the library and mingle with the inmates. He let me arrange the seating of the inmates into groups, and he allowed me to assign my interns to various tables in the way I wanted.

On our first day in the classroom I explained to the convicts how I wanted them to write poems and recite them. After demonstrating several alternatives, I said I was also curious to know if they could sign and if so, could they translate a poem they wrote into sign language.

As I spoke, they sat still with immobile features. I knew they were appraising my every gesture, weighing every word, mulling over whether they should trust me with their life experiences. After all, words carry our feelings and pains and joys, and they had been violated by so many officials from the common policeman on the street to the judge to prison guards. Why reveal themselves to me? Why open themselves up?

I started out something like this:

"There's nothing I can say to win your trust, to make this writing workshop successful, to make it work for you. There's nothing I can say to lift you up from the silence you carry within and disarm you of your concerns enough to express your dreams and pains and loves.

"But you have to do it, trust me. I won't exploit you, I won't hurt you. I'll respect your experiences. And there is no such thing as too bad, too horrible a thing to write—express it, make it into a song we can all share.

"You have an obligation to do this, a responsibility to let all those young kids hustling on the street know that it is okay to express and share and write and read your heart out to others. Wail it, scream it, sing it, cry it, but get it out and let the world hear you.

"Teach me how to see you, how to know what your hands felt when they were crushed and broken under boots, teach me your loneliness when your father left you and your mother abandoned you, teach me how to understand you, to see the dark and the blood and the fear of your lives through your words, through poetry."

And they did.

When we were moved to the library the next day, we had more room to spread out and either Karina, Efren, or I could sit helping the inmates at each table. The whole time during the workshop we had two cameras filming, with the final cut to be aired nationally on *ABC World News Tonight with Peter Jennings*.

The guys got right into their work. I gave them a list of topics—love, hate, sadness, dreams, and so on and they plunged into each one with unabated eagerness. There was an urgency to their willingness to participate, and they were being open and trustful and cooperative.

Their questions were sincere.

"Mr. Baca, how do I write to my wife? How do I find the words to say what I mean? And especially to my little baby who I won't see for years?"

"Trust your words," I said. "Be simple, to the point. If you love, say 'I love.' Then put some details in—special times, special people, what the room looked like, the sky, the hour."

"Like, what if we just hung out on the corner, do we write about that?" another inmate asked.

"If the street corner was the center of your world, write about it. It's a lot more interesting than the darling worlds other writers write about. Aren't you a little tired of the darling books? Let's get real here. Going hungry is real, having no parents is real, being the target of racism and having no education is real; your life is filled with reality, sometimes sorrowful and sometimes happy, but real."

And that got them going. Hands sprang up with more questions.

"What about our guns or our crackhead fathers? Oh yeah, what about our dead homies?"

"Write about what you know. Great books are about what your lives are about. Problem is, you're letting others write about your lives. Don't you think it's time you step up and tell it like it is? Write about it. After all, you lived it. It's all about emotional truth, and *that* we need more of."

Then we performed.

One read a poem while another convict signed it. Another signed a poem to the class while the class wrote down what the signer was signing. It was unbelievable how extensive the language was. I had Crips signing to Bloods, the Mexican mafia signing to La Familia and the Border Brothers and the Texas Syndicato. Barriers disappeared. The space we worked in was hallowed and it gave no quarter to violence or hustlers.

And that was soon to be tested and proven.

We decided to have a public reading and all the participants in the workshop were pumped up to read before the inmates from outside the workshop. We took the liberty of inviting groups of convicts from several cellblocks to listen to our poetry.

I had a Crip stand twenty feet away from a guy in the Mexican mafia and this mafia guy twenty feet from a Blood and the Blood the same distance from another gangbanger. I wrote down a line of poetry and handed it to the first guy. He signed it and passed it to the next guy; the other signers sent it on, each signing the same sentence in their distinct gang dialect.

It was marvelous.

The very last gangbanger read it aloud. "Some-day-we-will-live-in-peace-and-all-get-along."

As that last convict finished speaking, out of nowhere and surprising everyone, a young black Crip in the audience started yelling about how gangbangers were not allowed to share signs with outsiders, how showing signs was prohibited. He cursed and threatened me until a Mexican warned him to be quiet and stop being disrespectful. He kept going until the guards removed him.

I wanted to tell the young man that was our problem—secrecy, holding things in, acting like secrets were our strength when our secrets were really weakening us.

On the way back to my hotel that day, I could still hear the black youth's voice and his fear in my head, "We can't be sharing our signs! They the enemy! They just want to get inside our code and then they'll use it against us."

It didn't matter if he was right or wrong. By not participating in a community exercise, he was depriving himself of communicating with others, isolating himself, denying himself this shared experience. Denying himself what allows us to be human.

The next morning he was found dead.

A Mexican came to the writing workshop that day stating he had to excuse himself from attending anymore. When I asked why, he said he loved the writing workshop so much he didn't want to bring bad energy into the room or corrupt the sanctity of the refuge for others.

"You see, Mr. Baca, when we share our feelings and dreams and pain, it's like sacred to me. I never got to do this, and it felt, like, it felt holy, you know. It made me feel like I was important, like I had some purpose. People were listening to me and I don't want to spoil that by bringing in bad energy for what I did."

"What bad energy?" I asked him.

He stared at me for a moment and then walked off.

And I understood what his eyes had told me.

The Embrace

On the last day of our stay at the Chino Correctional Facility, Uncle Jimmy threw a ceremonial sweat for us. We made our way to Uncle Jimmy's office, picked up a few sacred items and his medicine pouch, and then headed to the Native American Sweat Lodge, placed off in the corner on the main yard. It was surrounded with a high cyclone fence collared with coiled razor wire. A scruffy patch of gleaned brittle cornstalks befriended us in the way that an old summer garden gives of itself and then welcomes us back in a seasonal ritual of turning over the soil.

Inside the fenced enclosure, off to the side, were concrete showers where Valentine, Efren, and I changed into bathing suits Uncle Jimmy had given us. Then we walked across a little patch of parched grass into an area with leafless, gnarly elm trees lurched halfheartedly over a willow-branch-and-tarp sweat lodge.

About ten yards to the left and center of the sweat lodge, fifty or sixty convicts stood, naked except for the shorts they wore, stationed around the pit. Someone had started a big bonfire at the far end of the pit where dozens of volcanic rocks were reddening hot in the flames. The three of us slowly circled above on the rim, greeting each warrior encircling the pit.

There were many Chicanos with roots deep in Mexican tribes like Mechica, Nahuatl, Mayan, and Aztec. Each warrior handed each of us a gift—beaded bracelets, turquoise medallions, leather braided belts, and the like. They were beautiful, but even as my arms brimmed with heaps of gifts, I was stunned to see a blue-eyed, blonde-haired Indian. There were Asian and black Native Americans, too. I never knew they existed, but they did. They were standing before me.

After setting aside the gifts, we all entered the sweat lodge and Uncle Jimmy began the sweat by asking the Rock Carrier to bring in the rocks. He decided to start with twenty and when those rocks were in the sweat lodge, we began to sing our individual tribal songs. One by one each man stood in the darkness before the glowing red rocks and sang.

Each of the remaining men entered the sweat lodge until we formed a circle inside three deep. All sat, the first circle closest to the glowing rocks, enduring the excruciating heat, then the ones behind them in the second circle, and then the third bank of men against the tarp nearest the back.

When the last man had entered, Uncle Jimmy closed the tarp flap and all went dark, except for the glowing circle of rocks in the center.

A drum sounded, a rattle, and Uncle Jimmy's voice growled as if from the deep end of a faraway cave in Earth, uttering incantations that grew rounder and louder until it seemed we were all standing around the sun and hearing it slur out sweet rhyming vowels and growled consonants.

With each song came another hot volcanic rock until there were twenty-five, and then thirty. The whole time we sang and sang until all the rocks were brought in and the tarp flap closed permanently.

Uncle Jimmy sang and poured water over the red hot lava rocks. Then more water. More hot steam filled the dark confines. More song and more steam until my flesh felt like it were afire.

The hotter the lodge, the more we sang. Some men moaned and grumbled in agony; others writhed, trying to escape the scalding heat. Some wept aloud. Others yelped at the stinging pain. We all were experiencing the fragile flesh wrapped around our bones and heart. How vulnerable; how humbling.

And still Uncle Jimmy did not lessen the steam. During every song he scooped the ladle into the pail and refreshed the hot rocks, which sizzled with steam and made the men groan in agony.

Still hotter and hotter.

The steam represented the Creator's voice and presence, how the Creator manifested in the beginning when the universe consisted of numberless luminescent ribbons streaming in primordial infinity.

Steam was the Creator's breath. Steam was the way God spoke. Steam was the shape and form of our souls. Steam was the smoking mirror of the universe.

Valentine went on his belly behind me and started pawing the ground, gasping at the dirt, trying to suck oxygen from the soil. Efren curled up on his side behind me and endured the pain with clenched fists. I reached behind me in the dark and took each of their hands, and with their hands firmly in my grip, I sang louder and louder until my voice lofted above the others like a hawk looming, solitarily sailing on an updraft near the cliff's edge, its flight my song that drifted around the bodies of each man in the sweat lodge.

Uncle Jimmy then reached his tongs into the fire and grabbed a small red stone and pressed it against my back, bonding me to these men, now brothers, fusing me to this moment in time forever: a moment I would wear on my skin.

I gripped Val and Efren's hands tighter and sang, made the bonding go deep into the realm of soul bark, circle after circle to the core of deep bark, first year living bark, back-when bark, to the beginning of forest bark, and first hawk flight time.

But the best was yet to come.

No one was allowed to leave the ceremony, but one man started to wretch and heave and, begging forgiveness for breaking ritual, pled that he had to leave or die. When the flap opened and he left, I saw something that to this day still spreads a healing salve over my heart—as light came in from outside, my eyelids opened to see fifty convict-warriors surrounding me, embracing each other. I had never seen such a sight, men holding onto each other in the truest sense of what it means to love as men and affirming themselves as humans.

I had been looking for a cure for a long time, a cure that would heal myself, break through the brainwashing I had endured serving twenty-one years in the system—from orphanage, to detention home, to county jail, then on to Montessa Park for teenage gladiators, and finally to maximum-security prison. For more than two decades growing up, I had been taught to use my body as a weapon—that the flesh was a shield and a weapon to wound and scar and wield in battle.

This body, I learned, was not something in which one's heart thrived; nor was it a benign receptacle for feelings, or something a lover caressed. It was to be used to tolerate beatings, endure brutal afflictions, and then carried into the next wasteland arena of corrections abundant with hate, oppression, and institutional racism.

Eyes were to be crushed, mouths shattered, ears ripped off, tongues slashed, skulls crushed. We were taught this. To survive, one had to do it. Violence was the body's truest mate and bedfellow.

But for me, after leaving that life behind, I had a family, a wife and two sons, and I grieved privately that every time I went to hug my babies some horrible alarm went off in me and sounded the cruel alert that my body was not to enjoy a familial embrace—it was a warrior skin. For years and years I could not hug my children and feel calm and filled with love or feel that special warmth that comes with hugging one's children.

Until I saw these men in the sweat lodge hugging each other.

Their courage and sincerity healed me and moved me forward into another level of my own life. When I arrived back home after the sweat lodge and my sons picked me up at the airport in Albuquerque, it was the first time in my life that I hugged them and I didn't feel ashamed or awkward.

I felt loved, with the capacity to love in return.

Teddy Boy

He was the best dog I ever had and I've had a lot of them. He was a jaguar dog—that's what the boys down in the south called their Catahoulas. He had one black and one white eye, short tawny hair with black circles all over his pelt, a passion for kids, and enough ferocious heart and loyalty to disarm a whole army of thieves and addicts. And he loved to eat, to herd anything that flew, walked, slid, slithered, ran, or swam.

For him, an orchard or a field of crop corn was paradise, providing the ultimate pattern for his life, everything in its place, corner to corner, all bunched up inside the fence lines. This is where he loved to be, where he thrived.

He was ever so funny at times, and no more so than the time we were invited to a ceremonial sweat in Deneland, or Navajo country.

My two sons and I piled into my '65 Chevy and they begged me to bring Teddy Boy and I did. There's not much I won't do to make my kids happy, and I considered their request harmless; it would go a long way toward making our trip enjoyable. If they got bored all they had to do was look in the truck bed at old Teddy Boy, jowls puffed in the wind, ears pulled straight back like tawny ribbons in front of a fan, tongue slurping the side of his face, happy as a cartoon character pushed off a cliff and sailing down to his inevitable doom.

We took off at dawn. It's a good five-hour drive from Burque to Deneland and we pulled in around noon. Skins on the rez walked down dirt roads, some on horses, others in beat-up trucks, bicycles glued and wired together, or horse-drawn wagons.

This was real rezland, not gentrified by whites or brand-new adoption agency buildings, there were no clean BIA cars or great basketball players or musicians. Just a lot of open and endless prairie, horizon to horizon, land and scrub brush ending only where it met the sky. All around, no matter where the eyes roamed and set, lay open eternity.

Now and then, we'd drive by a corral, a hogan, a small shack, and a horno so old they seemed to be in possession of a genuine spirit, one that could talk to you if you dared open up and risk a conversation with the adobe wall or mesquite stick in the corral fence.

Then, joining us almost at the same time that me and the boys turned off a dirt road and geared uphill, toward a corral and a whitewashed cinder block bungalow, with a huge teepee next to it, and a large community overhang set in the middle of two structures, from every direction in the vast space of cacti and sage, filling me and my boys' hearts with awe and our eyes with surprise, were more and more Skins bouncing along dirt roads in cars and trucks, coming from all directions.

It was ceremony time.

We got down from the truck all happy and excited, and Teddy Boy jumped out and dashed off before any one of us knew it. He was gone as fast as a lizard.

Elders and medicine men had come from all over—Canada, Mexico, and the southwest. It was Dene country, and the man leading the ceremony, the Main Healer Man, in his nineties, was honored by all.

One of my sons sat to my left, my other little boy to my right. There must have been forty people in the huge teepee, all males ranging from ten years old to over a hundred. Sitting around the sacred fire, we drummed, we sang songs, and drank peyote. Long into the night, one by one, each person stood and recited his story. And we sang, drank peyote, and drummed.

At some point during this long night, I felt something firmly nudging my butt. The pressure was coming from outside and I knew immediately what it was. I knew with horror, with anger, and with fear what it was: it was Teddy Boy, who had returned from his adventures, Teddy Boy who had returned from fighting other rez dogs and had survived it.

Despite my anger, part of me was proud of him. Rez dogs are famous for pack fights—ten against one. And since Teddy Boy was from the city, they had jumped him; I was quite pleased that he had lived to bark his tale.

However, I was also, with my son beside me to my left, spiraling through a magical galaxy far beyond this known Earth and solar system, accompanied by my animal spirit, and having drunk so much peyote, I was in a serious vision.

In and out of my vision I went, prodded out by Teddy, then back in again, then pushed out by his nose. I was sure that after awhile Teddy Boy would smell me enough to be assured I was inside the teepee and safe, and that he would recline next to me outside of the teepee, licking his paws or wounds until I came out.

But the unexpected happened, as it always does.

Main Healer Man stood up and announced he was going outside to smoke with the moon, to offer up sacred medicine, and sing. And outside the teepee, as he started chanting, I began to hear the dreaded growl. Deep and low, it punctuated the Main Healer Man's sonorous and somber appeal to the Creator.

Swallowing hard, I inhaled and tried not to look around. I knew that the others were glancing at one another with concern.

Then it happened: snap, bark, and growl, snap, bark, and growl.

I'm in deep shit, I thought. This cannot be happening, not with the *main* Main Man.

Main Healer Man entered the teepee. "Whose dog is that?" No one answered.

"Whose dog is that?" he asked again.

I kept my head down in shame and mumbled a song. And when I did look up, it was with a disgruntled look. With false shock, I eyed everyone. Who could have been so dissolute and irresponsible? Not to mention disrespectful!

But then Teddy Boy came back. Violently, he nudged then prodded the cloth of the teepee at my waist.

And then they knew.

Soon the sun rose and the ceremony ended.

The men shook their heads at us as they exited the teepee. Kids pointed at me and laughed. My sons and I walked toward our truck, while Teddy Boy, oblivious to our shame, happily leapt up at our hips, joyous at our emergence.

Yes, I was thankful Teddy Boy was not killed by other rez dogs, and that he had not been executed by warriors when he threatened the Main Medicine Man—but I was still going to teach him a lesson.

What lesson, I was not sure.

He was a herding dog. The best. He loved the clusters of orchards, the symmetry of wheat stalks; any pattern that had a herd symbol was his paradise. Maybe I would tie him to a huge cottonwood tree in the fall and watch him yowl in excruciating frustration as the wind blew and scattered million of leaves through the air before his eyes.

Complete disorder would be his undoing and my revenge.

Repo Man

Some of my fondest memories are of when I was five years old. That was when my Uncle Santiago would come over to Grandpa and Grandma's house, stamping his work boots outside the screen door, and enter the kitchen where the woodstove crackled and popped piñon nuts. He'd lean against the kitchen counter, twirling a toothpick in his mouth, and he and Grandpa and Grandma would share the latest news until he finally announced he was there to take me with him for a few hours.

Then we'd go, and I'd ride shotgun in his old faded green '51 Chevy pickup. It smelled of bags of livestock grain and hay bales, and the old bones of the truck springs and chassis would groan at each rut and rib, hoes and shovels clanking against the fifty-gallon drum sloshing with leftover lunch slop he'd picked up from the local high school.

On the outskirts of town we'd pull up to his small piece of land to feed the pigs and his one crazy mustang horse, which, one day, he dared me to ride. I did and promptly got thrown, much to my uncle's delight.

Then we'd head back to Grandma's, dogs barking at the bumper and chasing our tires. I'd never been out of our small town, and to me it was a ride around the world. Many days, I'd walk to his house and spend the afternoon outside in his front yard sitting on the running board or the hood or playing in the truck bed of that '51 Chevy.

When I was fifteen or sixteen and living in Albuquerque, my dad drove up one day in a big shiny Buick with gleaming trim and a butcher-block bulkiness. The front bumper had two polished missile heads protruding, and centered between the cones was a chrome grill as bad and beautiful as shark's teeth.

My dad was a drunk and almost every day he'd let me drive him to the neighborhood bar and then back to his boarding room. The Buick was spacious as an Arab palace and armored like a submarine: big radio knobs, massive steering wheel, heavy doors, hubcaps so elaborately designed they could have been in an upscale art gallery, green-tinted windows with a blue stripe across the top. It was an awesome statement of American brawn and bravado. When you saw it coming down the street, it purred, *I am God of the road.*

My dad was often so drunk that I'd cruise around first, showing off to my friends who'd be hanging out on stoops or streets. Then he'd rouse from his alcoholic stupor, unsquinch his eyelids, and blearily moan, "Go home."

It was not long before I bought my own car and it was a doozy—an old Studebaker station wagon. I had to keep my head out the window when driving it to keep from dying from monoxide poisoning. There was a bad, bad leak in the muffler somewhere and most of the exhaust came inside. But I could live with that because it was my first car and first cars are like first loves—even if it was coughing on one leg and leaning on a cane, it was a prince in my eyes.

My second car was a Hemi—don't even ask me why I bought it; I guess, though, the word *Hemi* induced all kinds of fantasies in my head of being the baddest dude on the road. I thought it would be the ultimate panty-dropper, but it turned out that I could only go from zero to ninety, nothing in between. I hopped from stop sign to stop sign for a week until I gave it away for a hamburger and fries.

There were a few more cars but suffice it to say I knew nothing about cars, didn't know how to tune one up, didn't know one motor from another, makes and models all blurred into one nameless thing called a car. I was never infatuated again with automobiles until decades later, when I was in my thirties and I walked into the Galles dealership on San Mateo, in Albuquerque.

There, was a green LSE Isuzu SUV, top of the line.

It was a showroom shocker, gleaming like an emerald necklace, and the friend I was with convinced me I could actually get it despite the fact that I had the worst credit in the world. In fact, if you looked at my credit report, you might have a stroke and choke to death.

Poets don't have credit. They give accountants nightmares and bankers secretly wish all poets could be dumped on a desert island and abandoned. Why? Because poets don't make money, don't respect money, and scoff at credit scores. Poems, you see, have no monetary value. And in my mind, you only get good credit by surrendering your soul to Wall Street pirate idiots, who have no soul or dreams or passion. I've always despised the credit system, and purposely never participated in it.

So I was in tenfold shock when, after filling out the paperwork—as it was, playing along in a make-believe child's game—the salesman came out and handed me the keys.

I was like, what the hell, you *serious*? I thought something must be wrong with the capitalist system to let a poor poet have this four-wheeled yacht, but at that moment I thought, hey, maybe God is directing this comedy—and who am I to criticize the main, main MAN?

I drove that baby out of the showroom, the first poet probably in the history of mankind to drive a car that classy freely out on the road. The babes stared at me with false love when I came to a traffic light and guys envied me when they saw me drive down the street. Open mouths gaped at me and I was clocking it all.

A couple years later I missed my first payment and I experienced the bite of the capitalist vampire fangs.

I couldn't believe these people! I called them and told them I was going to be late and they threatened me and ordered me to turn my SUV over to them.

"Look," I said, "I already paid twenty grand on it and no one is taking it from me, especially when you threaten me. It's unjust, immoral, unethical, and evil. You ain't getting it. End of story."

But it wasn't. *They* were accustomed to writing the end of stories.

However, they were dealing with a poet and they'd find out that it was going to be like going into a dark hole in space. When one tries to take a beautiful machine from a poor poet, the fight is on.

A company collector started calling me every day to ask about my payment. I told her I would make it, but a little late. She asked me when I came home from work, where I lived, and where I parked. She made me suspicious and from that point on I parked in the garage.

For a time, I continued making payments, but then I missed one. The same woman called, this time saying that a representative from her company had gone to my house and found I no longer lived there. She needed my new address for billing purposes, she said, so I gave the address and apartment number to her.

"Are you home right now?" she asked. She wanted to send the representative to see me.

"Yes." Actually, I was at the airport waiting to board a plane.

"Well, can you hold?" A second later she was back on. "My driver doesn't seem to see your apartment. Is the vehicle there?"

"Yes," I said, enjoying the deception now. "I can see your tow truck, and I'm right here."

"Hold on." I heard a click, and then another, and she was back again, "You sure you're there? You see our truck?"

"Of course I do. It's right there. Well, now he's leaving, driving around the parking lot."

She called again, saying the driver couldn't find the vehicle. I said I was looking right at the Isuzu and it was parked right outside my window, but there was no truck and no driver.

"Are you sure there's not a truck outside?"

"What kind of truck?"

"A tow truck," she said, and explained they had to repossess the vehicle. There was nothing she could do.

I acted like I was in complete agreement. "Absolutely," I said. "But I'm looking at my vehicle and I can't see any tow truck."

She put me on hold while she went back to the driver and described to him exactly where I lived. When she returned, I told her I had to go and I hung up and boarded my plane.

This cat and mouse game lasted for a couple of months, with me innocently pretending to help them repossess my Isuzu, always playing dumbstruck by their near misses to encounter my vehicle.

I never heard from her again.

Another collector from a different company called. Although I never picked up the phone and actually talked to him, this guy was mean. He left threatening messages—that I was going to jail, that my credit was ruined forever, that there was no escape.

He'd start in the morning on the message machine.

"Ain't nobody getaway from Big Dog Maloney. I want that car." His voice was raw and gravelly like a smoker's. "It's that car or your you-know-what—I'm coming down to git it, hear? To git it. Ain't never lost a repo and don't plan to now—."

Oddly, I started enjoying the company of these repo people, listening to them deceive and threaten, twist and wrangle a million ways to try to get that car.

But what power did they have? I had no credit, so what was the point of threatening me with bad credit?

Just when I tired of one repo collector, another one would call. Sometimes I'd pick up and listen a long time to an endless sermon of benefits I would enjoy if I only turned in the vehicle. When they were finished, I would terminate the phone call by saying the same thing I always said before hanging up.

"You will never find it, never possess it, and never see it. You should have never threatened to take it from me after I paid so much already."

"I can be real kind to you, Mr. Baca," one guy said. "I like you. Bet you like baseball. Ever play baseball? I know you are an honest hardworking human being. Where you at anyway?"

I got into the conversation, knowing all along he was trying to sucker me into giving up the goods.

"Now I'll talk to my boss and get him to modify what you owe," he said. "I'll get that down from what—23K—how about 15K today and we call it square."

"Sure, sure, you think you can do that?"

"Lemme see, I'll call you right back." And after he told me that his boss agreed to have me pay only 15K and the car would be mine and how he was pleased as an unbroken egg yolk, feeling yellow-eyed-under-the-sun-good and how we should one day take our families fishing, I told him:

"I can't do it."

His gooey mishmash hardened into dried clay. I could picture his face, big eyes wide with rage, face pale corpse chalky.

"What do you mean you *can't*? You done made a deal."

"I know, I know, but I thought it over—can't do much more than five hundred dollars. That's it. Think about it. Call me back tomorrow morning."

One company handed me off to another company and they started getting smarter, even though the company names got dumber—Pitbull Repo, Resolution Repo, Rambo Repo, and so on. So when my eldest son decided to travel across America, I gave him the Isuzu to tour in. It had about twenty thousand miles on it at this point. When he returned it, it had gone over one hundred thousand.

After that I passed it down to my second son and he used it as a dune buggy, going out on the sand dunes west of Albuquerque and driving it off hills and into gullies to see how much air he could get under it.

It was turning out to be one great recreational vehicle.

When it wasn't being used by the kids, I kept it at a junkyard on South Broadway, over at Big Tommy's place. I'd go down and use it when I needed it. The collection calls kept coming and it was nice to have them call; I was on their mind and it made me feel needed and wanted.

I'll never forget the last guy to call on the Isuzu. He was from Denver and I told him the truth—the Isuzu was parked at a friend's house in the mountains and he could pick it up if he wanted to. It had been parked up there for a long time and thieves had stripped it down, taking mirrors and lights and stereo. He kept trying to bargain with me, offering deals: pay only five thousand and we'll call it square.

In between each proposal, we talked about his dreams, his health, his problems, talking for close to an hour. Each time we ended our talks with me saying the same thing. "I'll think about it."

He was such a nice guy that I finally offered him three hundred dollars and we'd be even. He was startled by the low offer and tried to get me up to a thousand, and I told him on second thought, fifty dollars. I gave him the address, told him it was stripped down, but perhaps by parting it out he might get a hundred bucks.

"Yeah man, check it out—don't feel so bad, man," I said. "The sun's gonna rise tomorrow and you're going to have another sucker to play off of. You might even make your rent for the month.

"And I'll tell you," I continued, "parting stuff out ain't that bad. Shoot, once I parted out my uncle's dead dog, claiming the bones were voodoo talisman from a powerful voodoo person and I couldn't stop people over at the flea market from paying triple above what my price was. Crazy huh? They sure like parts."

I never talked to him again, no one ever called again, and the Isuzu still remains parked in the mountains. It's actually become quite useful. The last time I checked on it, birds and rodents and insects have pretty much made it theirs. There's no way I can take it back now; it belongs to Nature.

Oh, and by the way, I now own a beautiful bicycle. I ride it all over town on errands. And it not only gets me to where I have to go—I'm much healthier.

Didn't Mean To

I'd been coming in regularly to see a group of teenagers locked up in the Bay Area. Some of them had committed crimes so serious they were heading straight to prison from jail, for around six years.

Many of these kids, against the ropes for one reason or another—parents who were drunks or addicts, bad neighborhoods, bad schools, lousy teachers, cops—believed the good life couldn't happen to them. They didn't allow themselves the hope that one day they could have a nice pad, genuine friends, or warrant respect and self-esteem for work they might do. To them, that seemed about as likely as the possibility they might invent a cure for cancer.

So I was never more excited to see these boys than I was now, to share my good news.

We had done an experiment earlier in the year. I'd told them I was going to write a book of poetry about them and I'd asked them to line up later that night, at exactly eight o'clock, in front of their cells. I returned a few hours later with a photographer, James, and he shot them standing at the bars. We used that night shot of them at the bars as the cover for *C-Train and 13 Mexicans*, a book of poetry published that year.

The book was about them, and they were blown away when I returned to hand them each a copy. It completed the circle for them, from telling them I would do it, to writing the poems, to it being sold nationally in bookstores. They couldn't believe that their lives were actually meaningful enough for someone to write about. It got them thinking. For some, it even got them dreaming themselves out of their habits into a new, vivid, and socially engaging life.

When I walked into the jail that afternoon, I was as heady as a kite on a windy day, fancifully flighty with the news I'd gotten earlier in the week, the news such a surprise. My publisher had called me from New York to tell me that *A Place to Stand* had just won the International Prize at the Frankfurt Book Festival in Germany.

I went into the room and looked around. These were high-security kids serving time for murder, drive-bys, dealing crack, and robbery. Guards stood at the back and to the sides and they were cool guards; they'd always taken part in my conversation with the boys, listened intently, and conveyed to the kids how important education was.

And the kids knew how important it was to read and write. For years, it had been my life's work to teach inmates to read and write, and to try to make prison more humane for the next generation. But as I looked around that day, I realized I was fooling myself. The celebratory tidings I'd brought in with me paled as I confronted reality. It had been almost a year since I had been back and I didn't like what I saw or felt.

The group in the room was divided into races—Chicanos/ Mexicans and Native Americans on one side; Crips and Bloods in another corner; Asians and Whites in the middle but separate. The kids had that look in their eyes, that glare of hurt mixed with rage and glassy defiance. What had happened during these nine months to raise the scale of hatred between races so high?

The room felt like a fight had just occurred, invisible blood all over the walls and floor. It hurt my heart. Young, beautiful black and brown and white faces stared at me. I gazed back at them with wonder and pain and confusion. The answer, dear God, the answer. What could redeem these kids in society's vindictive eyes? How could we save their futures with a punishment other than the man-made hell called prison?

"What happened?" I asked.

They stared coldly at me.

I nodded, and said aloud, "I see, it's that again. Up in my face, talking smack, one dis gives rise to another dis, until it breaks down to killing." I shook my head. "What a waste. What a waste of the lovely lives of the very, very smart kids that you are."

I paused a little and said, "Let's talk about violence. I see you all are hating on each other again. Everything I've said, it's all wasted, wasted words, wasted feelings of respect for you, wasted dreams. You all like to waste, don't you? I don't. I don't like wasting my time or my belief and faith in you—lot better people than hustlers and jokers and pretenders and haters to worry about than you. So if you decide to get real, you tell me, 'cuz I don't wanna waste my time with liars and punks."

"We ain't no punks," someone said.

"Well, let's see, first of all, simple question—how many of you have at least one parent?" (All raise their hands.) "Should we talk about how we hurt them and they're the ones who stuck by us?" I said. "Punks hurt the people they love. You all know that, and you all know you're smarter than most kids. How many kids—the rich, the privileged, the trust-fund snobs—can claim to have your life experience?

"You've been through it all—sorrow, loss, joy, ecstasy, challenge, conflict, life-and-death issues. Come on, you were given what most kids only dream about. You lived it.

"And so you made bad choices that landed you here. That doesn't mean you lost the gold of your life experiences. That simply means you're still waiting to figure out how to use those experiences and that wisdom and that learning that makes you now so smart.

"So let's do it now."

They all looked at me with those adorable but unmoving masks one has to wear in jail to protect oneself.

"How about a letter to someone you love. I'm not going to tread on sacred ground and piss you off. But I want a letter to the girl you loved and left out there. But first let's talk about that love, define that love, describe that love."

That was when we got into their girlfriends, and the scalding-hot idea of what it means to be a man.

How does one live up to what a man is in America? Conventional opinion would say a man is enterprising, has power, makes good money, has status and respect. But these teenagers had missed the boat.

In trying to find a little respect for themselves they'd committed crimes; in search of their manhood, they'd ended up in jail. Most didn't have fathers or paternal figures they'd looked up to in their lives—they took as their mentors street corner crack dealers.

To them, a man never backs up, defies authority, isn't afraid of dying in the streets, and will shoot if called upon. Peers judge them by how far they're willing to damage their lives and destroy their futures:

Deal with it.
Punks cry, men don't.
What, you can't handle it, chump?
Never back up, dude.
Never admit you feel pain. Your body is a shield, a
weapon, and it don't feel nothing.

Don't ever snitch. Go down for a brother even if you didn't do it.
Handle your business, even it means doing life in prison.
Do what you gotta do, by any means necessary.
Get chics. Don't be a punk—gotta have a bunch of chics and control them, manage them.
Get your respect by violence and selling drugs.
Put in work for the crew or your posse by selling drugs and making money.
Always carry a gun.
Recruit the young ones in the neighborhood, soldier up.
Be down for your gang and homies.
Right or wrong, you be willing to give your life to the crew.

This was the kind of advice they got and the code they lived by because of the social vacuum in which they existed.

These kids don't share any of our experiences: they never came of age, they were born men; they never left home because they never had a home; they have no idea what education or schooling has to do with career or life; healthy relationships don't exist and the hint of one terrifies them; they were born dead, live as dead men, and so death is welcomed when it comes to get them.

Here's how they think:

Prison ain't nothing. I'm going and I'm ready.
There ain't no such thing as a *kind* me, I'm bad and I'm mean.
I work for the deal. I'm a hustler.
No cop or guard is cool, they all chumps that need messing up.
Women ain't nothing but fine flesh.

All kinds of ways to get around the system.
I don't need to change and no matter if they bury me in
prison. I ain't changing.
The world treats me like I'm nothing and I'm treating it
like *it* ain't nothing.
I'm a straight-up gangster.

How was it possible, in light of this kind of thinking, to break
through to their feeling selves and make them drop their masks?

I told them I wanted each of them of write me a letter and
address it to me, since a letter and a person in mind would allow
them to write more easily. I said I wanted them to tell me about
the girlfriend they left behind, how they loved her, how they'll
miss her, and the nature of their relationship with the girlfriend.

We talked briefly before they started and one said, "She's my
b . . . and she'll do what I say."

It got a laugh from the classroom, and another kid offered,
"They the reason I'm in here. I should of given her a wake-up
slap . . . but I was too kind. . . ."

And from the corner of the room came, "Once you let a b. . . .
get all strung out on your dope you don't have any dope and you
can't trust her anymore . . . 'cept for booty calls."

"My woman knows she belongs to me 'cuz I treat her good—
I'm there to fend off any predators. She relies on me, you know?"
one said.

"I don't play no bullshit—she's mine, I own her."

Another one added, "Yeah, I tell her she do what I say, I'll
take care of her. And she does."

"My baby knows I love her, and she loves me. She does what
I say when I say and it's because she's mine. Even though I do
what I want to do with other girls, she's mine, she belongs to
me."

One of the guys up front in the first row of chairs said, "Mine'll wait for me as long as it takes for me to do my time. I gave her some fierce loving, everywhere and anytime. When I wanted it, Daddy Mac laid down his power staff."

He got a lot of supportive *yeah*s from the class.

After the letters were written, I discussed a common theme in the letters—that they take what they want from their girlfriends when they want it. They wrote that they took her body when they wanted it, had sex with her on a whim anywhere, and that their girlfriend was expected to give it when they demanded it.

I told them that what I was about to say was going to scare and piss them off. First, I accused them of raping their girlfriends. It was the stupidest thing they ever heard, they replied, they really loved their girls and what they did on car hoods and under park trees was love.

"Wadn't no rape—that's how she likes it."

"You have to rough 'em up, show you love her."

"That's all they understand on the streets."

"I seen my momma's boyfriend beat her so I beat mine. That's love. I don't know how it is up there in la-la land, Mr. Baca, where you come from—no disrespect—but on the streets the first punk along trying to snatch your lady, you got to teach her that she can't do that."

"Yeah, enforce the rule of domination!" the last kid said.

I told them to brace themselves and that I meant no disrespect.

"All of you are headed to prison and when you get there, sooner or later someone is going to try and rape you. The rapist is not going to ask for permission, he will take what he wants when he wants it. The rapist believes the victim loves it, expects it, and should give it whenever he demands it."

One big boy said, "You outta control Mr. Baca. You gotta chill."

But I continued. "The rapist will treat you the same way you've treated your girlfriend."

Eyes glassed over with rage: defiance and attitude, violent intent.

Slowly, a heavy pall blanketed the room as they made the connection and their eyes tried but failed to keep strong emotion from pulsing into them. They felt the predator's breath on their necks. They felt vulnerable. I told them the emotion they were feeling was the emotion their girlfriends felt when they mounted them for sex. Helplessness. Fear. Compliance under silent duress.

Then I asked them to write a letter to their girlfriends, asking for forgiveness and describing how they really felt about them and explaining how absolutely sorry they were for ever hurting them by forcing them into sex.

Many were weeping as they wrote their letters.

Many got up to use the bathroom but it was really to blow their noses while they secretly wiped away tears.

Years later, one of these kids sent me a letter stuffed with grimy dollars and pocket change. He wasn't dealing crack anymore, and he was still going to the community college. It was all he had, this gratitude money. He explained: coming back late one night from the community college library, he found his mother tearing their apartment to shreds looking for crack. It was the psychotic frenzy that afflicts addicts when they need a fix.

He left disgusted, hurt, blaming the horrible world for his mother's condition. He walked around Oakland for hours trying to lose his sorrow and when he returned he found his mother in a corner, reading a book of my poems that I'd given him when he was in jail.

She looked up from the page and said to him, "I want to go to treatment."

He wanted to thank me for coming to jail and seeing him all those years ago, and I was deeply moved by his gratitude.

At Stanford University, where my archives are kept, I wonder what graduate students doing their doctoral thesis on my work will think when they come upon this grimy envelope with crumpled dollars and pocket change. More importantly, if my young friend continues school and makes it to Stanford University, and he finds it himself, I'd like to include a note in the envelope for him:

Go out and buy yourself a nice meal, my brother, you've earned it.

Birdhouses

I was truthful in what I had just said to the group of women I'd been working with in the Grants Prison, located in Grants, New Mexico, but stunned by the question that followed.

For three months I had been bringing a documentary crew to film our writing workshop and every week, as the women trusted me more and more, they disclosed the horrors of how men had treated them. No—I should change that word, from *horrors* to *torture.*

And I couldn't take it anymore.

So I told them, "Look, no more stories about men burning you, beating you, about fathers and uncles and mother's dates raping you, no more blood and cuts and overdoses, and bleak and horrible events and incidents. Let's write a bit about more happier things."

But they had none.

That's when the woman asked, "If we can't write about our families, then what the hell do we do? You're the teacher. We can't just make shit up."

For a couple of weeks I thought about what she had said and then I came up with a solution.

I didn't know if I would be permitted to do it but I was going to try anyway. So I drove down to Santa Fe, to the offices of Cabinet Secretary of Corrections, Joe. He was a good guy, from the

South Valley where I was from, and he had given me plenty of leeway to do my documentary project.

But when I asked him to be allowed to bring birdhouses in to the women, and also to be allowed to paint them together and set them around the prison, he balked.

"What the hell you trying to pull?" he said.

When I explained my reasons and plan to him, he cautiously and begrudgingly agreed.

"But if anything goes wrong," he warned, "it's the end of the writing project."

The following week when I met the women and told them I was bringing in birdhouses, they seemed elated. I didn't tell them what my plan was, just that we were going to be doing some serious writing, and serious didn't mean somber and tragic, but celebratory.

I've always kept my word and this was no different, just a little harder. The day of the workshop, the guards had to check out not only the camera equipment and such but the birdhouses and paints, and when I walked in, I was a little bit late. Not that late, but it didn't stop the women from scolding me—until I told them I had a surprise.

"Remember I told you I couldn't take the grief any more? No more asshole men making you hold drugs, punk-gangsters busting you and your kids . . . no more?

"Well, come on up here and pick out your birdhouse. You're about to have new families."

I had no idea how powerful this was going to be. The women took the birdhouses and started painting them according to their cultural ethnicity. African American women painted their houses

African style—yellows, blacks, reds, tribal symbols. The Chicanas did their houses in Mexican colors—green, yellow, red, and loaded the walls with murals from their tribal affiliations: Mechica, Mayan, Incan, etc. The Caucasians followed with Appalachian and medieval colors and motifs.

The one thing they had in common was that they all wept and wept as they painted their birdhouses. I mean really wept. Tears poured down their cheeks and streamed into the paint, discoloring the original pigment with salty tears of passionate forgiveness.

They were feeling in themselves their primal innocence again, experiencing early dreams they hadn't allowed themselves to remember because the pain of betrayal had shattered their childhood hopes.

This ritual of creating a new beginning was their personal baptism, cleansing them of their previous sorrows and reinvigorating their faith in the goodness of themselves.

The next week we set up the birdhouses outside the prison building but inside the fenced perimeter. We agreed that whatever birds arrived at their birdhouses, this was going to be their newly adopted family. For weeks after that, the women monitored their specific birdhouse and soon their journals filled up, page after page. It was impossible to keep them from writing.

The women acted like expectant mothers, chattering about their new child, about a new father, about the wonderful bird mother. Hawks, blackbirds, sparrows, owls, and other birds appeared at the birdhouses and I had a lively flock on my hands.

The women became effusive and enthusiastic and were impossible to contain. They laughed about their children, about the habits of their bird mothers, how cute and lovely they were, and so on. The women learned about nature writing, about describing the sky and the Earth, but in a very real and connected way. They reconnected to childhood feelings and embraced the sparrow as if it were an angelic messenger with a specific tiding to enrich their hearts with joy.

Then one day, while reading to the women good examples of descriptive nature writing by John Muir, Edward Abbey, and another page from Turgenev on landscape, Lonnie rushed up and declared with alarm, "Maria's in trouble."

I ran to her "home" and found her kneeling on both knees cradling a bloody but very dead sparrow. A red-tailed hawk a few houses down had killed it.

There was very little we could do to console her—dead is dead. It's a facet of life we learn to accept since we cannot avoid it. Maria and some women dug a hole under the birdhouse and buried the bird and prayed over it, wishing it a good journey into the beyond. Maria and a couple of her friends walked back to the classroom and I stayed with the other women outside.

We talked about unforeseen accidents and our responses to them. How we deal with death, how we have to relearn how to grieve, how we have to embrace the community in our grief, publicly admit our loss, be unashamed to let others view us in our darkest hours.

We talked about how not to hide our loss, mask it in pretty clothes and nice cars, subdue it with drugs, numb or cauterize it with blatant bravura as if the tragedy didn't happen to us, as if it didn't affect us at our deepest core. And right in the middle of this discussion, while I was using St. Francis' life as an example, a woman cried my name out from the education building.

"Jimmy!" she hollered, waving me toward her. "Maria's lost it."

I flew toward the building and as I entered the classroom, I saw Maria hurling a chair against the wall. I also heard guards coming down the hall and when they were just about to plunge into the room wielding clubs, I begged the captain to please let me calm her down.

The captain motioned the guards back and I began to talk to her softly.

"Maria, death jolts us into a frailty that allows us to glimpse our beauty. Loving through sorrow is a great gift—it's a powerful incentive to love those who are alive. Death allows us to renew our efforts to appreciate life. It's through our sorrow we become known to ourselves."

Though it sounded like unapproachable philosophy, she understood my words and the emotion behind them.

Maria and I sat together for a good thirty minutes, with the rest of the women in the background, slowly inching their way forward until they surrounded us and we all crowded in and held each other in a communal show of trust and empathy.

Shortly after this incident, the State of New Mexico contracted the Corrections Corporation of America to take over and administer the prison. Their first move was to destroy all the birdhouses.

The Warden

I was invited to come to Phoenix, Arizona, to give a keynote speech at a conference on prison reform. It was a national conference, attended not only by correction reformers but wardens, cabinet-level secretaries of corrections from different states, security staff, and educators in the secure setting areas.

A woman from the Justice Department informed me she was bringing a new study on prison reform—statistics, new methodology, alternative punishments, community engagements. I was intrigued, but when I arrived she met me in the lobby and handed me this four-inch-thick collection of data to read.

"I believe you will be very interested in the direction corrections is going. We're developing some very unique approaches to rehabilitation," she said.

It had never crossed my mind that I'd have to set aside months to read the study. For me, prison reform was pretty cut and dried—you cannot rehabilitate anyone without community involvement and education. I took the huge tome to my room, threw it in my suitcase, and promised myself I'd skim it over for essentials in the coming months.

I got ready to give my keynote for the conference and later that afternoon took my seat at a table for lunch in the conference hall. There were about five hundred people there, all excited about sharing and networking and renewing old contacts and making new ones.

Before I was called up, the emcee gave recognition to those hard workers who had made the conference possible and then he announced they had a special guest in the audience. It was a warden, who was being honored with a gold watch for fifty years of dedication in performing his duty as a warden at several prisons.

I looked at the old man hobbling up to the stage and thought I recognized him. Perhaps no. I knew many wardens from the many prisons where I had given innumerable writing workshops since my release.

I walked up to the retired warden and gave him a free stack of my signed books. He shook my hand with genuine gratitude, and I slapped his back in a friendly fashion, offering congratulations. I then went up to the stage and proceeded to speak about prison reform, what I believe works and doesn't work.

"If you dehumanize a person in action and environment," I began, "words to humanize him will never work. If you send a man to school in the day and allow him to get gang-raped at night, what good is the education when the man has lost his will to live? If you reward a bully with extra desserts at dinnertime because he beat someone up, and mock the man who refuses to fight, you spread the venom of unconscionable violence into our culture and society and promote it as a way to live. If you design a place that praises what is evil, then expect evil acts. This is what prison does, has done, and will always do.

"Prison is as traumatizing as war, as life destroying as addiction, as community breaking and family destroying as a killer on the loose. Except that the killer will one day be free and enter your home, abduct your child, addict your loved ones, terrorize your peaceful life, and take the life of innocents.

"We must confront this social scourge called crime, and deal with criminals in a way that they will stop committing crime. We must change it, and to do that we need the community involved."

In the middle of the crowd, the retired warden sat with his gold watch, about twenty tables deep, right in my line of sight. And as I spoke, who he was and where I knew him from hit me with the force of a lightning strike.

He was my warden.

But not only was he my warden. He was the one who had me escorted to his office, the one who had hit me and vowed *on my death* that I would work or die.

I could still hear his voice. "*No one* in my prison gets away with not working," he'd said. "I'll bury you out back in an unmarked grave if you don't work."

Did he remember the afternoon years ago when he charged from around his desk, pit bull–stout, looming over me, huffing with rage? From the side of my left eye, I'd seen a blur, and a second later his fist had smashed into my cheek.

This was the man who had sent vicious inmates down to my isolated cell to fight me. This was the warden who had sent goons down to my dungeon cell to beat me.

And why?

Because I wanted to attend GED classes and he said I couldn't. He ordered me to work; I refused. And because I refused, this warden kept me locked up in isolation month after month. For the remaining time I spent in prison, I was never permitted to attend school and I continued to refuse to work.

And Lord have mercy, how The Creator works in mysterious ways indeed—some fifteen years later, he was sitting right before me.

I did not know if I should tell him who I was or not. Was it not enough that I should have a dozen books published and be in such demand as a speaker that my calendar for each year filled within weeks? Was it not enough that I was now a poet using my life to free and heal spirits and write poems? Had life not already rewarded me a million times over with an abundance of poems, friends, family, and fame, while he had spent his time locking people up—had in a very concrete sense spent his life locked up by his own choice and willingness?

You could see it in his craggy and wrinkled face, in his eyes that had lost their light. His soul's death reeked with the stench of a rotting carcass. He sat intently listening to my words when I simply couldn't restrain myself any longer from sharing what I knew with the crowd.

Directing my voice and eyes to the warden, I spoke. "Do you know who I am? Do you remember me?"

He squinted and pinched his brows together, shuffled through his old finger-worn deck of memory cards and shook his head no.

"I'm Jimmy Santiago Baca. I was in your prison at Florence for six years, and you vowed I'd never see daylight unless I obeyed you and went to work."

He seemed confused.

"Seventy-two to '78. You had me put in the dungeon for years. I remember you brought me to your office one day and because I had a red ink pen in my pocket you badgered me about loving blood, and had the guard, what was his name . . . oh yeah, Five Hundred, hit me from behind while I sat in the chair looking at you."

He got it. His face turned red and he stood and swept the books off his table. Then he walked out.

At that moment I realized how good it felt to have someone *else* have to walk out of a room. For many years I was the one walking out, and now it was the warden who walked out and I who stayed to finish my speech.

All my life, from classrooms where the nuns told me to leave for misbehaving, to wanting to say something and being hushed or ignored, to being a no one, unknown and unimportant, to being chased off my indigenous lands, forbidden to speak my language or practice my rituals in public—always, I'd been chased off and ordered to leave.

And now he had to leave the room and I stood tall and empowered and spoke from my heart.

Life deals you a beautiful hand to play from time to time.

Saving the Tree

I admit it might have looked like a dumb move on my part if you value only money, as many people do, but sometimes enough stupid moves pile up to make a tidy little karmic stash—and even a few happy days.

It started when I was in the market for a house. Well, before that. It began when I arrived home one night from reading poetry and found my house on fire. Dozens of boxes of journals and writings, first drafts of poetry books, scores of characters and events and experiences I had written about, all with the hopes of one day spending serious time maturing the kernels into good poems, were now on the floor smoking in the ashes.

Yes, it was terrible. But in a sense it was also a relief.

For a long time, I had wanted to carry my notebooks to the trash and throw them away, but I feared I'd be tossing out work that might be good. I'd been harboring my early writings out of insecurity and when they burned, a weight lifted from my shoulders, freeing me with courage to start new work.

That night as I rummaged through the debris, hoping to salvage family photos, a neighbor of mine came over, a gangbanger named Chris, and handed me some cocaine, tequila, and a joint. I thanked him, but declined. Walking through the charred house, bidding good-bye to my past, I felt secretly refreshed the fire had taken the old writing away.

Shortly after that I was riding the back farm roads of Los Padillas when I found an old, crumbling adobe house with the biggest American elm tree I had ever seen standing nearby.

I fell in love with that tree.

In fact, I parked my car in the tall, weedy driveway and checked to see if the farm gates were open. They were locked, so that afternoon I slept in my car listening to the huge branches of the elm sway lightly in the breeze and feeling the immense loving and compassionate presence of this grandmother tree.

When I woke and asked the neighbors who owned the house and land, they told me "a crazy woman." They pointed to a two-story house at the end of the dirt road, surrounded with handsome fields heavy with green alfalfa.

They said that the house was falling down and uninhabitable, that the floor and walls were caved in and infested with mice and field rodents. There were even weeds growing up through the floorboards.

Nonetheless, the next day, I parked at the gate again, walked down the dirt road to her house, and pushed the red button on her cyclone fence gate topped with barbwire. Into the intercom, I stated my name and reason for wanting to talk to her. The gate slid back on wheels, and I went up the steps. She greeted me at the door.

She was rich. She owned many acres all around, including the decrepit adobe a few fields away. Thin and haggard with a cavernous face, heavy jaw, and scrawny voice, her eyes peered rather than looked. As kids, my friends and I would have called her a witch.

I told her I wanted to buy the house next door and even she admitted only a dunce would want to buy it. She was intending to destroy the house, hire a dozer, and raze it.

"That nasty tree," she spit out, "I'm going to chop it up into stove pieces and burn it this winter."

Being rich, I guessed, the tree was an economic problem for her—its roots would one day fracture the foundation of her house, or the branches would crash on the roof one windy night and cost her money she wasn't willing to spend. For me, it was a beautiful gift from the Earth.

I told her I had a little money, not much, and I was anxious to ask her the price. When she said $90,000, I had to breathe in with effort to keep my composure. It was way more than I could afford. My only hope was to come back and see her and beg her to lower the price.

When I told the neighbors the price she quoted me, they laughed.

"You're not foolish enough to pay that are you?"

I was. I had my heart set on it.

Many gasped, wide-eyed and open-mouthed, shaking their heads, certain I was insane. "It's all falling down, how you going to live there? You're going to spend more money fixing it up than you will paying for it."

Still others used the rich lady's quote as evidence of her mental incapacity. "That just proves my point—she's plumb nuts."

I was still going to buy it. Not for the house, but to keep the tree from being cut down. I would find the money somehow.

While my brother and I worked to rebuild my burnt house with the insurance money, I couldn't get the tree out of my mind. It kept calling to me, entering my dreams, penetrating my thoughts each day. In fact, I went down there daily and looked at the tree. One day I climbed over the fence and stood next to it and embraced it. Embraced a part of it, that is, since it would have taken six adults holding hands with arms extended horizontally to encircle it.

Hugging it, I could feel the energy in the bark that sizzled in every inch. I could feel its massive roots below me, going down perhaps hundreds of feet; there were movements in the roots, a presence like breathing in the dark. Most of all, I felt the tree look down on me from its towering height and bless me, acknowledging my affection for it.

With each of my visits, this feeling that the tree was alive and sensitive to my love intensified, becoming stronger and stronger even in my dreams.

I believe in things that have no foundation or basis to believe in and likewise with the house. I was out in the yard carrying lumber and just about done rebuilding my house that burned down. My brother was a carpenter by trade and a good one, and out of the ashes of the old house, he had constructed a beautiful new little home. We were both admiring our work when a stranger drove up and asked if I was selling it. I asked him for a price he thought was fair. He gave it and I accepted. Life is strange; sometimes it brings you just what you need.

Within a month I was moving into the adobe house. And many an evening I sat on the porch and reflected on the tree and me. We had something between us—a joy, a somber grace, an understanding.

That elm tree became my symbol of strength, a symbol of endurance, a reminder of how the rich lady had wanted to cut it down as so many people in my life had wanted to cut *me* down.

Yet both of us had survived.

In some way we both understood that. We were two friends trying to restore our hope, live with dignity, and for me, trying to heal the lightning-strike wound of being homeless, both believing the sun would rise at dawn and we'd have another chance to grow.

Interview with Jimmy Santiago Baca

From Chicano down-and-out street tough and maximum-security-prison denizen to poetry slam champion, holder of the Wallace Stevens Chair at Yale, and recent winner of Germany's most prestigious International Award, Jimmy Santiago Baca has led a most unusual life. Filled to the brim with great pleasures and sufferings, harmonies and contradictions, his breathtaking poetry, fervent memoir, sharp-sighted short stories, social dramas, and other creative work are a testimony to this and form an important cornerstone to Chicano/a and American letters today.

Born in 1952 in New Mexico to a Chicana mother and an Apache Indian father, Baca learned swiftly and suddenly the pains of not belonging. After his father died of alcoholism and his mother packed her bags for California, the young Baca found himself first living with his grandparents and then deposited in an orphanage. After years of growing up within the walls of the orphanage and dropping out of high school, Baca hit the streets of Albuquerque to find solace with other like-minded, deeply alienated Chicanos. Barely getting by and treading deep the streets of cities scattered throughout the Southwest, in 1973 he found himself charged with possession and intent to distribute drugs, and was sentenced to a six-year lockup in a maximum-security prison in Florence, Arizona.

Four years of isolation plus electric shock treatment did not break Baca's spirit. Indeed, Baca turned his internment into a self-fashioned chrysalis: starting from scratch, he first learned how to read and write; subsequently he applied himself to master words and aesthetic forms, and ultimately he devoted himself to become a creator with both. All along this unusual apprenticeship he never lost sight of his one and only goal: to use the power of literature to build new worlds, new meanings, new emotions, and new interpretations in order to help his readers reach a position from which the actual world could be perceived under a different light.

With a GED tucked safely under his arm, Baca walked out of prison ready to face the world as a self-identified Chicano poet. Baca's *pinta* (prison) poetry resonated loudly with audiences inside and outside of the state penitentiary. While still in prison, his first poems saw the light of day in *Mother Jones*, and a year before his release he published his first chapbook, *Jimmy Santiago Baca* (1978). In these early poems, his already exceptional lyrical voice speaks out against the dehumanizing conditions of prison life. The year of Baca's release from the penitentiary in 1979 also marked the publication of his first collection of poetry, *Immigrants in Our Own Land and Selected Early Poems*.

In between working as night watchman, janitor, laborer, and numerous other jobs, Baca had to fight against his own demons (drug addiction and alcoholism) and to find inside himself the resources to continue writing. A new chapbook of his appeared, *Swords of Darkness* (edited by Chicano author Gary Soto), and then a second book, entitled *What's Happening?* (1982). Baca was promptly becoming recognized as one of the great new Chicano poets, albeit a controversial one.

In 1987, Baca published *Martin and Meditations on the South Valley*, a semiautobiographical poem about the epic journey of the orphaned Martin across "countless towns" in America and the eventual finding of roots in family and home. *Martin* won the American Book Award, and in 1989 it was followed by the publication of the *Black Mesa Poems*, in which Baca continues to portray the rich lives of Chicanos and Chicanas.

While Baca is mostly known for his poetry, he has also availed himself outstandingly of other means of expression: in 1991 he brought out a play, entitled *Los tres hijos de Julia*; in 1993 he wrote a screenplay entitled *Bound by Honor/Blood in Blood Out*; and more recently he published a collection of gritty realistic and magical short stories, *The Importance of a Piece of Paper* (2004), and a novel, *A Piece of Glass* (2009). In his memoir, *A Place to Stand* (2001), he tells in lyrical prose the story of his life. Baca continues to write in Albuquerque. He also works with at-risk youth and convicts nationwide through his nonprofit, Cedar Tree, Inc.

Early Life

Q: You have had a pretty rough life. Let me just run through with you some of the things that have happened to you. You were born of both Chicano and Apache descent. Your parents divorced and abandoned you when you were 5 years old. Why did they abandon you?

JSB: I guess the reason they abandoned me was that they didn't know how to take care of themselves. They were being assaulted and assailed from all sides. Well, you know, when that happens, how can you cope with taking care of kids when you can't even take care of yourself?

Q: How did you end up in an orphanage?

JSB: I was taken there because the authorities thought it was bad influence to be around the people of my Pueblo. They thought that I should learn how to speak English and be a Catholic.

Q: So you left the orphanage when you were twelve? Did you run away, or did they release you?

JSB: Well, I ran away a lot of times. I had this problem, as Nerudas says in one of his poems, I had "little tiny flames" shooting out from my heels . . . as most children do. They were going to send me to Boys Town, and I ran away. Ultimately, I just never came back.

Q: Where did you live? How did you live?

JSB: Well, you know, I hustled. . . . I really depended on the kindness and the generosity of my people. And I lived with many friends and families. They would give me a meal and they would give me food. The hardest part about living on the streets as a kid is when the rest of the kids are in school, and the grown-up adults have gone to work, and you are left with the very ancient, or the handicapped, or the invalids, you begin to think there must be something wrong with you, too, that you're one of the damaged ones.

Q: Did the chaos of your childhood teach you how to risk?

JSB: Yes. At almost every turn in the road, I had to face my fear. "What will be this person's response if I confront them? If I admit I don't know something? If I show how scared I am?" There's an organic order in the chaos around us that you have to find. It's in the apparent chaos of nature, this order. Poetry helps me find that order in myself and then everywhere around me. I find order in the saddest sorrow.

Prison Life

Q: How did you end up in prison? What were the charges?

JSB: Drugs, possession, with intent to sell, to distribute.

Q: Once you were in prison, did you have any goals or were you just trying to do your time and get out?

JSB: I wanted to go to school and the counselor promised I could go to school if I didn't get in trouble, so I worked 60 days in the kitchen, getting there at four in the morning. It was a beautiful experience to go out that time of morning. I'd stand in the yard until the guard came and got me. I would look at the moon and smell the desert smells. It affected my soul in a big way. My dream was to go to school and learn how to read and write and then go back to villages and work with kids.

Q: So, did you get to go to school?

JSB: They reneged on the deal and betrayed me, said I couldn't go to school. When that happened, something broke down in me in the reclassification committee meeting. They said, "You're going out in the field." I couldn't get out of the chair. I remembered being hit by this guard named 500. The last thing I saw was the room whirling. He had hit me so hard that I had flown out of my chair.

Q: Why did they call him 500?

JSB: He was over 500 lbs. He broke all the ribs on my left side. He broke my jaw. They had to wire my jaw back together. Any type of defiant behavior like that has to be dealt with immediately. Here was a convict who was saying he wanted to go to school and for some reason the committee thought that was more dangerous than stabbing somebody.

Q: What did you do?

JSB: I went to my cell and refused to work, and the repercussions of that one decision sent off a frenzied current of confusion, not only through the homeboys I was in a gang with, but the guards freaked out too. The warden came down and said, "If you don't start getting in line, you're not going to walk out of here."

Q: What happened then?

JSB: They sent Mad Dog Madrill. He was the one person you did *not* want to visit you.

Q: He was a guard or a prisoner?

JSB: A guard.

Q: What happened when this brutal guard came in?

JSB: He pulled me out of my cell and took me to isolation. As I was standing on the landing and watching them tear my cell apart, other convicts all started throwing stuff at me. I tried to disassociate myself from myself and say this is not really me. Someone threw hot water, and someone threw urine, and someone threw feces at me. It's even hard to talk about. I wiped it off. I turned around and I kept saying to myself, "They're not mad at me; they're mad at somebody else." All of a sudden the guards came and chained me up and walked me out of the cell block. I'll never forget this feeling when I walked out; I was suddenly filled with an overwhelming sense that I had wanted to do this since I was born. I just wanted to make a choice in life, whether it was right or wrong. It gave me this overwhelming peace or purpose. It was like I had a role in life.

Q: How did you survive? Did they put you in the hole? Did they brutalize you?

JSB: For three years they knocked the living hell out of me. They broke a lot of bones and I became somewhat of a hero because I lived in administrative custody where they called me a security risk. The guards would come down and beat me, but I would fight them and then wake up in isolation.

Q: What did you do down there during the long days?

JSB: I was reading so many things. I was not really in prison; I was some place else. They had left me alone by this time and they had put me with the death row inmates. It's great to be near the death row inmates because they read the really great books, not comic books, you know? They are preparing for the next world.

Q: They didn't want to waste their time?

JSB: No, they didn't want to waste their time. I was reading *For Whom the Bell Tolls*, Fitzgerald's *Great Gatsby*. I asked myself, "Who kept this from me? Why didn't they give this to me? Why did I stray off and float like flotsam along the beach? I have a right to read; this is my legacy as an American." So I was reading voraciously.

Q: Did you begin to write then?

JSB: Well, the first poem I wrote I stole out of the Bible. I replaced the words so I could send a poem to a woman I was in love with. I gave it to this guy named Bonifide to read and Bonifide said, "No, you can't steal from God." He hit me with the biggest challenge I'd ever faced: "You've got to be honest, Jimmy." When you're a street kid, you can't be honest. Especially if you're in love with a woman; you have to tell her the car is yours, even if you stole it. If you admit to yourself that you have nothing and you are no one, the next step is suicide. I couldn't go there. So, I wrote a poem saying that I had nothing but this poem to give her.

Q: You sent her the poem?

JSB: Yes. Then, believe it or not, someone came to see me. I thought it was my brother, but it was Teresa, the woman I was in love with. She'd come all the way from Chicago. A *poem* made her drive half way across the U.S. to see me.

Q: What was it like to see her after all that time?

JSB: When I saw her, it was devastating because I knew I didn't love her anymore. I had been reading books like *Madame Bovary* and they had changed the DNA structure of how I saw and defined beauty.

It's so sad, a sad thing, when the literature you've been reading redefines your standard of beauty, and the one thing you've been living for is taken from you. I had to make a decision about whether I was going to go out and be a criminal and wreck havoc or pursue literature and find out what was beyond this change.

Q: How did you make that decision?

JSB: When I walked across the yard, I was elated and yet in sorrow. I was experiencing the power of literature. It had actually changed my mind about something. I went back to the cell and wrote a poem to the judge to see if he would release me, but it didn't work. (*Laughter*) By the time I got out I had had my first book of poetry published, *Immigrants in Our Own Land*.

Learning to Read and Write

Q: When you first came to prison, you really couldn't read?

JSB: Well, no, you know, functionally illiterate. Anybody can read *it* or *you* or *a*, *and*, *but*. It's not so much the fact that you can read or not read. I couldn't read, but it's what happens to an individual who is not able to read. What condition does that person fall into?

Q: Did it ever bother you before then that you couldn't read? Were you embarrassed by it?

JSB: Never embarrassed.

Q: So how did you start to read?

JSB: Well, there was a guy named Harry, who was a good Samaritan in Phoenix, who wrote me a letter asking what I needed for Christmas. You know, he picked my name out of a hat and said, "It's Christmastime, you don't have anybody to visit or anybody to visit you, so what would you like?" And, I told him, "Could you send me a book, an English and Spanish book?" And he did.

When I began to read, I began very slowly, and I had these books that had English and Spanish on opposing pages. The material was very rudimentary, elementary, kind of religious teachings. Now what happened was that I would read most of the day and into the night, and I would pronounce the language aloud. I pronounced adjectives and adverbs and nouns and prepositions and so forth aloud, and then early in the morning I would wake up and begin to write in a journal.

Q: What sorts of things were you recording there? Words, thoughts, feelings, memories?

JSB: I was writing things that I remembered doing as a kid and as an adult and so forth. And what happened was that, in a place like prison where you are deprived of all sensory enjoyment, language became more real, more tangible than bars or concrete, than the structure of buildings in the landscape. So I began to read, to read and write in the sense that, metaphorically, I wrapped myself in this cocoon of language, and when I came back out, I was no longer the caterpillar: I was a butterfly.

Q: You used your newfound literacy in prison to help other convicts?

JSB: I started writing letters and poems, and reading for the convicts. They gave me coffee, cigarettes, pencils and tablets, and I started a very thriving ordering system.

Q: Do you remember anything you wrote, any of the letters or poems that you wrote for other people inside?

JSB: I remember the first stanza I ever wrote in my life. I was naked in the shower. I was in prison, and I think I was reading Turgenev. I soaped myself up, and all of a sudden I got hit with a lightning bolt. You know how they call it the "muse"? I call it the "Mohammed Ali left hook." These lines came to me, and I ran out of the shower naked and the guard hit the alarm button, because you can't run, you know?

Besides, there goes a naked Mexican running down the hall, what are you going to do? He hit the alarm button, and I ran into my cell with soapy hands and stuff, and wrote down these six lines of poetry. And then of course, the soap got in my eyes and reality came back and I had to rush back to the shower to wash the soap off. But at that point I think I was classified as a nutcase.

Q: Do you remember the lines?

JSB: The poem was a response to a group of senators who had been touring the prison the previous day, examining the aftermath of a riot. The lines were "Did you tell them, that hell is not a dream, that you've been there, did you tell them?"

Q: Were you able to read it to someone after you wrote it?

JSB: Ah, no . . . except for the birds, the trees, and the air, the dust, and the sun outside my window.

JSB: My goal in life was to be an English teacher. So, what I was writing, I wasn't particularly gung ho about having people hear it, or even read it, because I didn't think I was a poet, I didn't think I was a writer, I was simply trying to grasp the language. And, in doing so, I kept a journal. I kept many journals.

Q: You first began to write poetry in prison, publishing in *Mother Jones'* literary section that was edited at the time by Denise Levertov. Why this magazine?

JSB: *Mother Jones* was doing the Black Panther inquiry, the killing of George Jackson in prison, so it was all over the prison. Some guy threw the magazine in my cell and said, "Hey, they're paying a hundred bucks a poem." I didn't know how to put the stamp or the address on the letter or anything, but I took my shoebox and grabbed a bunch of poems that I had written. And I sent them to a place called San Francisco—never expecting to hear back from them, but they published the poems internationally and sent me 300 bucks, and I was like, wow! I thought I could be rich off of poetry—that was a really naïve assumption!

Q: So, was the $300 held for you until you were released?

JSB: No. I put it in my store. I bought ice cream for all of death row and all of segregation. I just splurged.

Q: You treated everybody?

JSB: Yeah, since everybody had been supporting me for a few years, I decided it was my turn to give them something. That was one cold day in hell.

The Power of Language

Q: You love language, you say. You've called it almost a physical thing for you.

JSB: Oh, I love language. I love language. Language, to me, is what sunrise is to the birds. Language, to me, is what water is to a man that just crossed the desert. I remember, as a boy, grown-ups looked like huge redwood trees to me in a storm, or they looked like boats without a map in a bad storm at sea. And the grown-ups in my life were always caught up in dramas. And the one thing that they all had in common was they couldn't express that storm inside of themselves. And I was so caught up in that drama that I vowed one day I would grasp hold of the power that could evoke their emotions. For me, at least, I wanted to know how to say what was happening to them and I wanted to name things.

Q: How were you able to find the power of language in prison?

JSB: I had been writing poems to the convicts' daughters and wives. One day a stone straight-up killer came to my cell and said "I want you to write a poem to my mom up in Alabama." I said it would cost him a carton of cigarettes. I wrote it and it was my first opportunity to go into that place where my mother had abandoned me at five years old. I went back to that period and I remembered playing with my mother's hair. I got so deep into that poem, it shook every tendon in my body. When the killer came back to my cell, he said, "Read it," because he didn't know how to read. As I began to read the poem, I noticed his knuckles turned purple on the bars and his face was turning red. That's not a good sign because he could kill me. I wondered if something happened in the poem where I had insulted his mother. So I handed it to him and said, "Take the poem," and he said, "You read it," and stared at me with a glazed rage. When I finished reading the poem, he said something I will never forget. He said, "How does a Mexican know what's in a white man's heart?" I knew right then and there I had a power that was endless.

Q: Did the other convicts sense this power?

JSB: Well, when I would read to the convicts, there was a sense of awe, my awe, their awe, and at the same time a sense of vulnerability, of my, our vulnerability. In other words, language had such a tremendous power, and then, in many instances with convicts, language was the very tool that had been used to destroy them and their families.

Q: How?

JSB: For example, when their mothers and fathers had gone into offices to ask about taxes and didn't know how to speak English, they were assaulted with English, by this same language. It was their mothers and fathers who had gone to courts and not understood the English language and were too proud to ask for interpreters. You see, the pride of these people comes from the fact that they had been living on this land for anywhere from 500 to 2,000 years. They had a direct family lineage of living on the land, and of the many catastrophes and tragedies that occurred in their lives, one could trace most directly to their inability to understand the English language.

Q: The ability to access language, then, goes much deeper than simply knowing how to read and write?

JSB: A remarkable thing occurred to me when I came upon language, and I really began to evoke language to de-create me and then to give birth to me again. What I experienced was this: when you approach language in this being-reborn sense, you approach language in the way that the Hopis approach language, which is that language is a very real living being. I approach it as if it will contain who I am as a person. Now, when language begins to work itself on you and make certain demands of you, it begins to ask you to risk yourself and walk along its edge.

Q: Which is what happened with you.

JSB: Which is what happened with me—I gave birth to myself.

Q: Did language have this potential for you all of your life?

JSB: I can distinctly remember when we didn't have anything to eat, as a child, when my grandfather would begin to sing all these songs. And the songs slowly but surely would end up taking our hunger away.

About Writing

Q: So, you developed your own sense of language. I mean, you had it obviously with you, but you began writing and reading in a kind of personal effort.

JSB: I had a blinding reverence for life in its loving form, and I had a blinding terror of life in its violent form. And I found myself literally scattered between those two poles of terror of life and love of life, that language I began to beckon and beg. I began to beg like a dog at the back door of words. I would beg that these words give me sustenance in the same way we feed our body food. Please give me something to live for, and it was that cataclysmic faith, it was the Armageddon of love and faith, and all of that. The idea of fatality, that life will end today, and I must have one truth, and it really literally could have because I had contracts on me to be killed because I refused to quit writing and so forth. Well, I begged that I live, or at least let me say one thing in life, let someone know I was alive, let someone know that Jimmy Santiago Baca came to Earth. Please let me leave something.

Q: What were your models at that time for being a poet?

JSB: What sustained me through the darkest periods, when I thought I might die, when I was having nervous breakdowns, were the Mexican poets and the Spanish poets who unceasingly gave passion to the work, gave passion to the language. They didn't write poetry that said, "Well, I went down to the store. . . ." No, they said, "I MUST go to the STORE!" And it was at these weak moments when I felt myself fragmenting in my entire existence, falling away like sand through my fingers. I couldn't keep it together. It was falling away from me. I would passionately open up Pablo Neruda, Federico García Lorca, Jaime Sabines, and these voices would say to me, "Fight Santiago, you get up and fight, don't let the darkness take you. *Hijo d'su. Y despues de leer como un poeta como Neruda, me levante, y va uno recio adelante.*" To translate that, I said, after reading Pablo Neruda, I would stand up and give this hardy howl, woof, woof, come, I'm ready.

Q: I can see that in your writing too. Your writing is full of that kind of energy. Let's talk about how you write now that you have made your mark on the world.

JSB: I start writing and I write very eclectically. I'm sort of eccentric in the sense that I'll write ten minutes and get up, walk around, sit down, write five minutes, get up, walk around. I'll do different things according to what I'm writing. With *Healing Earthquakes*, I had a different approach. I sat down and just wrote passionately, a burst, a shower burst so to speak. When I'm writing something else like short stories or a novel, they each have their different approaches that affect me physically and that I follow physically. So that's how I do it.

Q: You enjoy each of those processes equally?

JSB: What we love, we have no control over.

Q: How do you perceive yourself as a writer?

JSB: One of the interesting things about being a writer in America is if you don't come with all the credentials, it's pretty hard to be comfortable calling yourself a writer. I wasn't comfortable until I was in my early 40s when I began to say, "I'm a writer." But, I still hadn't written *A Place to Stand*; it was still looming in the distance, saying, "You ain't nothin' till you deal with this." Since writing *A Place to Stand*, I have become very comfortable with the idea that I'm a writer.

Q: What advice do you give to young people who want to become writers?

JSB: When I teach in colleges or universities, I'm struck by the students' unwillingness to risk. It's debilitating to them, this fear. I tell them, "Don't write the way I write or the way Ezra Pound writes. Do it like a rock, a tree." But they're scared, really scared, and they can't do it.

If you really are a writer, then write. Writers write. They don't sit there thinking, "Oh, I need six more credits for this, and four more credits for that." Bottom line, writers write. They soak up everyday experiences then transform this into something else in the process of writing.

About Poetry

Q: How did you come to poetry?

JSB: I put the gun down and picked up the pen.

Q: How did poetry affect you while in prison?

JSB: I don't know if I would have lived had I not found poetry. The thing about poetry is that early on I came to it in prison in such a way that society was not going to accept me, so I then had to bring society to me through my poetry. I had to write the kind of poetry that was accessible and yet which would not compromise my experience, so that society would say, "Oh we understand what he's writing about, and we think that the poetry's okay." And my life has always been sort of like that, about unendingly learning about all the mistakes I made and never being so stupid as to not try to learn something new from my children or from the earth or from friends.

Q: What inspires you to write poetry?

JSB: What inspires you to breathe? If you want to live, you breathe.

Q: What influences you the most regarding your poetry?

JSB: Just the extraordinary sweetness of people, or the rage, or the hatred. I can't stand the comfort zone. So many people I know, their parents give them their homes, and they get married and have children, or whatever. That's it. They don't ever go beyond that. That's not what life is, you know? People say what distinguishes us from the animals is that we think. Well, then why the hell don't we extend some compassion to those under tremendous duress? What about getting into the whole melee of poverty and racism and violence and murder and drug addiction? Get in there, roll up your sleeves, and do something! I believe it's our responsibility as citizens to get in there and not accept the constant failure of prisons to deal with racism, lack of privilege, and impoverishment—to not accept any of that. Just get in there!

Q: Is that conviction something you keep going back to in your poetry?

JSB: Understanding is the key to everything. If I'm making a sandwich, and I'm peeling an avocado, as a poet I represent myself; and if I pay attention to what I'm doing with the avocado and I write a poem about the avocado, then representing myself is representing the avocado—I am the avocado. Poetry extends in ways that don't limit it. It gives you a brief view of the intense beauty of life.

Q: Poetry for you is in every moment?

JSB: It is in the canyons of the bone. I don't try to harvest my poetry from what happens in society's institutions as much as I try to reap the poems from what's happening behind the boundaries of society.

Q: You've said that when you were a young man in prison that discovering language and learning how to write saved you, that you were reborn through poetry.

JSB: For some people, prison actually helps them; they're told what to do, how to dress, and they accept that. Some people shouldn't be let out—they would create havoc in society. But when I was in prison, I realized that I had gotten caught up, that I didn't belong there. The only avenue of escape open to me was to plunge myself into language, into reading. When I did that, it was as if all the walls around me crumbled down, all the wire fences. When I found poetry, it was like being sucked into a shooting star. The epicenter of that attraction was that it taught me how to love myself. I saw how a poem could embrace a paltry, scared human being like me.

Q: Do you remember a specific poem that started this process?

JSB: Actually it was a story by the Russian writer Turgenev about a man going out in the morning and hunting that I connected with. Then there was Emily Dickinson, Ezra Pound. Dickinson had a self-imposed exile and isolation that I understood.

Q: Those writers helped you find yourself as a poet?

JSB: I always felt that there was this body that Jimmy Santiago Baca inhabited in the here and now but that there was also an ephemeral aspect of myself, floating beyond myself. Reading poetry connected with this. It was as if I had been wearing a mask, and poetry allowed me to put on my real face.

Q: The widespread response to your work, from Los Angeles to Boston, suggests that many Americans are in need of the healing power of language. Do you think that is true?

JSB: Corporate power has laid itself on our shoulders, thrown us into the rapids, carried us along so that we live in a state of constant desperation and confusion. We're fragmented, to a point of no return. We need spiritual balance. We need a way to hold onto one another. Poetry can provide that.

Teaching Life

Q: You know what a difference being able to read made for you. Is that why you work with the kids, the gangbangers, steelworkers, convicts, and illiterate adults?

JSB: Damn right. Right into the barrios and the projects and the poor white areas. They have such a reverence for language. They can't believe the language can carry so much power, and once they get hold of that, they begin to unteach what they were taught about who they are.

If they were taught to be racist or violent, language has this amazing ability to unteach all that, and make them question it. It gives them back their power toward regaining their humanity. That's why I do it. Not out of any academic or scholarly incentive.

Q: Where do you begin to "unteach"?

JSB: The whole thing is this: If you don't use just basic grammar, if you don't get the language down, you're not going to have access to a tool that people use as a weapon against you. The only reason I was never taught to read and write was because it was easier for them to lead me. But the second I learned to read and write, I began to lead myself.

Q: You believe everyone has a chance at life through language. . . .

JSB: Prisoners might be illiterate, but, boy, are they intelligent. Education is the key. There are proven educational models right now that are stopping recidivism, racism, and violence in prisons.

Q: How did you begin to become a teacher?

JSB: When I came out of prison, I was given the Wallace Stevens chair at Yale and I went there and also worked in New York. One Christmas I went back to Albuquerque and I gave out books; that's all I had to give. Every person I gave a book to would say, "What's this word? What's that word?" Then, a gentleman came up to me and said something that was really remarkable, that was sort of a reckoning, a pivotal reckoning. "Instead of being at Yale, why don't you come here where we need you? Because I don't know how to read." I went back to New Haven and told them I couldn't stay any longer.

I started my first writing workshop in Albuquerque at St. Anne's church, in a barrack behind the church; thirty years ago we had our first poetry workshop. Since then, I've gone back into prisons. We are working in a women's prison now, in McLoud, Oklahoma, with forty-one women who have committed murder. We are doing a documentary there.

Q: You have established a nonprofit for your work?

JSB: Cedar Tree, Inc., is my nonprofit and we do so much. Through the grace of God we get donations in the mail and we continue the work. We do workshops with homeless teens, inmates at Soledad State Prison, and kids in a juvenile detention center. We did a project at an unwed mothers' school called "Don't Hit Me" and then we did a project at the juvenile center where we tried to teach kids not to hit. We did it all through literature.

Q: You have said that your work with kids keeps your own voice strong.

JSB: I don't dismiss the academic and scholarly sectors of society. I go listen to what they say, and I read what they write. But it's not near as exciting as hearing language invented from experiences that have truly been lived, almost, in many cases, on the verge of dying. I've never heard a professor stand up and say, "I'll give my life for this," and yet I listen to these kids and they say, "I'll give up my life, I put my life on the line with this poem about my mom." And I'm like, "Wow." That keeps educating me about where my poetry should be.

Q: Is it hard to "break into" the lives of people with whom you work?

JSB: We put ourselves in places where we serve. When I work with at-risk kids who haven't had much education and I tell them I'm going to read them some words, and I see some smiles or a look of recognition as they respond to these words, this nurtures me. After a period of weeks, a trust, a familial attachment develops. We're one, we care for each other.

Q: You help kids become a part of a community.

JSB: We all want to be included. If I can go into a classroom and include this young girl, she also includes me in her life. I feel so empowered that when I leave, I feel I could open a door just by thinking about opening a door!

Q: How does literacy, teaching kids to speak, write, and appreciate literature, support this process?

JSB: There are all these divisions in our lives. When I go into the neighborhood, I see kids who despise anyone successful or anyone different than they are. I tell them, "This isn't being a man, spreading hatred of people who are not like you." But the clarion call of our day seems to be opposition, you must oppose something. Poetry melts these differences. Reading does it. I die every time I read a book. It's so wonderful to forget that I exist. I want to thank the writer for letting me in. I'm grateful that there are writers out there who can give me this. It's there, this salvation and redemption. All we have to do is pick up a novel or a poem to find this.

Q: You once wrote that in your teens you had become the coauthor with society of your own oppression. What are you coauthoring with society now?

JSB: I want to coauthor the lessening of rage in prisons and the racism and the addiction that's killing so many young kids. I've dealt with my racism. I used to hate blacks and whites. I used to hate my own kind. I've dealt with that. And with my violence, with drug addiction, where I used to be an addict because I couldn't deal with the pain. I have dealt with that in the most nightmarish loneliness and have come out the other end of that, healthy and whole.